ROME

IN THE HIGH RENAISSANCE

NORMAN
UNIVERSITY OF OKLAHOMA PRESS

ROME
IN THE HIGH
RENAISSANCE

THE AGE OF
LEO X

by BONNER MITCHELL

By Bonner Mitchell

Les Manifestes Littéraires de la Belle Époque (Paris, 1966).

A Renaissance Entertainment: Festivities for the Marriage of Cosimo I, Duke of Florence (with Andrew C. Minor) (Columbia, Missouri, 1968).

Rome in the High Renaissance: The Age of Leo X (Norman, 1973).

Library of Congress Cataloging in Publication Data

Mitchell, Bonner.
    Rome in the High Renaissance: the age of Leo X.

    (Centers of civilization series, v. 33)
    Includes bibliographical references.
    1. Renaissance—Italy—Rome (City)   2. Rome (City)—Civilization.   3. Rome (City)—History—1420–1798. I. Title.   II. Series.
DG814.M5   913.37′6   72–9277
ISBN 0–8061–1052–X

PREFACE

IN HIS GRAND WORK of general history *The Age of Louis XIV* (1751), Voltaire distinguished for "men of taste" four great ages of civilization: the Age of Pericles (and Phillip and Alexander) in Greece, that of Julius Caesar and Augustus Caesar in Rome, that of the Medici in Italy, and that of Louis XIV in France. These sweeping judgments, which conformed perfectly to the neo-classical taste of the eighteenth century, were repeated by traditionalist historians of the next century and are familiar even today to people who have had something of a classical education.

Voltaire's third period, with which we are concerned here, included the time of the early Medici in Florence as well as that of the Medici Popes Leo X and Clement VII in Rome. In Italy, however, the *"Secolo di Leon X"* has long had a special standing of its own, and in English-speaking countries, too, the phrase "Age of Leo X" was once well known. Now English-speaking scholars of art and literature are much more familiar with the term "High Renaissance," which, though broader, focuses to a large extent on the same period and on the Eternal City. I have

elected to use both terms in my title. Neither is chronologi-
cally very precise. The name "Age of Leo X" was never
meant to apply only to the eight years of Leo's pontificate,
1513–21, and its limits are vague. The High Renaissance
is also ill-defined—and its very existence disputed—by historians. My actual period of coverage, so far as such limits
can be set, is the years 1503–27, from the beginning of
the pontificate of Julius II to the Sack of Rome in 1527,
during the pontificate of Clement VII. It will be necessary
to allude often to events in years both preceding and following the period.

The reputation of all "golden ages" of civilization is
precarious in our century of skeptical inquiry, and the one
with which we are concerned has probably suffered more
from scholarly debunkers than any of the others distinguished by Voltaire. Conservative scholars, particularly
in Italy, still cherish the traditional august conception of
the age. Not very many years ago the great literary historian Giuseppe Toffanin, in *Cinquecento,* wrote almost
lyrically of the "triumphant reconciliation of the Renaissance with Rome" (that is, with the Christian tradition)
that took place in the Eternal City during the early sixteenth century. Such grand and satisfying ideas do not
stand unchallenged for long today. Thus Giorgio de' Blasi,
in a long refutation of Toffanin, argues that the literary
movement of the Renaissance took some wrong turns in
Rome during the time and that much of the creative energy
expended went for naught. Other scholars, such as Domenico Gnoli, have revealed the seamy side of life in the city
during the High Renaissance. Still others have pointed out
correctly—and much less significantly—that many of the
achievements associated with the name of Pope Leo X

belong at least partly to the pontificate of Julius II (whose reputation has tended to rise as that of Leo X has declined).

It is not the task of this little book to prove that the Roman High Renaissance and the Age of Leo X were a period of superior cultural accomplishment, but the fact of the book's being written for the Centers of Civilization Series indicates of course that I, along with many other scholars, think that they were. The weaknesses and failures of the age were serious indeed, as I shall have many occasions to point out, but it has two claims to greatness that withstand all skeptical examination. The first is its achievement in the fine arts. The masterpieces of Bramante, Raphael, Michelangelo, and many lesser artists are still there for us to see. The second quality of greatness is less evident at a distance. It lay in the general excellence of cultural life in the city, in an atmosphere of intellectual fervor and moral optimism reminiscent of Athens in the fifth century and of Rome itself in the best periods of antiquity.

In keeping with the spirit of the series, I have not endeavored to give a systematic history of the age, though events and sequences of events are often recounted. My principal object throughout has been to evoke the temper of life—moral and material—at one time and place, so that readers may have an idea of what it was like to be a resident of Rome in the early sixteenth century at one of the finest moments in the city's long and famous history.

I am warmly grateful to the University of Oklahoma Press for having encouraged me to undertake this study. It has provided one of the most rewarding intellectual experiences of my career. Research for the book was done at the University of Missouri Library, at the British Museum in London, at the Bibliothèque Nationale in Paris, at the Biblioteca Nazionale Centrale in Florence and, above all, at the Vatican Apostolic Library in Rome, whose collections of sixteenth century books and of scholarly works on Church and local history are without parallel. The work owes much to the courtesy and benevolent interest of librarians in all these places. Professor Torgil Magnuson, of the Swedish Institute in Rome, generously gave advice for the preparation of my map of Rome in 1520. I wish to thank warmly the Research Council of the University of Missouri at Columbia for having supported my project with a summer research grant in 1968 and with a later grant for preparation of the manuscript. And, finally, I am grateful to my typist, Miss Barbara Blunt, for her unusual patience and capacity for taking pains.

BONNER MITCHELL

Columbia, Missouri

CONTENTS

ROME
IN THE HIGH RENAISSANCE

THE NEAR PAST

NO OTHER CITY in the Renaissance was so concerned with its own past as Rome. The heritage of classical antiquity, first, obsessed the minds of educated Romans. For many people it was in a sense the most *real* segment of the past, certainly the one most deserving of study and emulation. We shall have many occasions to see that classical revival was the dominant theme of nearly all intellectual life in the city. But we must not forget, carried along by local fervor, that ancient Rome was known in a literary way, and not through unbroken living tradition. Too much time had passed, and the rupture had been too severe. No Roman family could trace its ancestry surely back to antiquity, though a number claimed to do so. Real memory, personal and collective, was of more recent times, of the city's experience in the Middle Ages and early Renaissance. That segment of Roman history, in contrast to the classical one, is rather poorly known in English-speaking countries—and even in Italy itself. In order to understand the momentum of events in the High Renaissance, we must first look selectively at some parts of the recent Roman past.

3

After the fall of the empire the dominant fact of the city's life had nearly always been the presence of the papacy. The wealth of Rome in the Middle Ages was never comparable to what it had been in the best days of the Caesars, but money came into the coffers of the Church, and a large number of people, Roman and foreign, were on the ecclesiastical payrolls. There was also, to be sure, a more or less self-sufficient native population who may have constituted a majority at times. Agriculture was more important than manufacturing in the local economy, and that is one reason Rome did not develop into a vigorous city-state comparable to Florence and Venice. The main reason was the presence of the popes. Even if there had been a numerous and energetic *bourgeoisie,* it could not have become dominant either in the city's economy or in its politics.

In the event, the wealthy members of the permanent Roman population were usually landowners and nobles rather than burghers. The two greatest families were the Orsini and the Colonna, a very different sort of people from the mercantile Florentine Medici. (And even in the fifteenth century Clarice Orsini considered that in marrying Lorenzo the Magnificent she had made a *mésalliance.*) The Orsini were Guelfs; that is, they tended to support the pope in disputes with the Holy Roman emperor, while the Colonna were Ghibellines and took the opposite side. The two families were traditional enemies and disagreed on other matters besides those of high politics. The strife between them disrupted the city for centuries. There were also many other noble and landed families, so that society and customs in Rome were more feudal than in the city-

4

states to the north. We may say, paradoxically, that they were less "urban."

The moving of the papacy to Avignon, France, in the early fourteenth century was a great blow to the Roman economy. The exile of the popes lasted for more than seventy years and was followed by the forty years of the Great Schism and by a further troubled period during which there was often still no strong pope in the city. It was only in the middle of the fifteenth century that a stable Church government settled again in Rome. During the more than a century and a quarter of papal exile and dissension, the city declined economically and demographically. Historians long thought that its population fell very low indeed—to eighteen thousand, some have said—but this extreme view is now disputed. (Petrarch wrote that it still had an "immense" population [*populum immensum*].) There was, in any case, little building during the period, and many structures fell into disrepair. The basilica of Saint John-in-Lateran was roofless for a long time, and the belfry of old Saint Peter's itself was left unrepaired after being struck by lightning. The area of the Republican Forum was called the Campo Vaccino ("cows' pasture") and the peak of the Capitolium, the Monte Caprino ("goats' hill").

It was, however, in this time of material decay that the spirit of Roman patriotism had its most remarkable manifestation. There existed a Roman *comune*, or city government, analogous to the governments in the thriving cities to the north. Relatively little is known of its history in the early Middle Ages, but its power was certainly subordinate to that of the popes and often to that of the local barons as well. Its offices may have been, indeed, largely honorific. Its seat was on the Campidoglio, as in the Renaissance and today. This government naturally tended to become more important in the absence of the pope. Then, on May 10, 1347, a young man, Cola di Rienzo, marched on the Campidoglio with armed followers, took over the hill in the name of the Roman people and read aloud a new constitution.

Cola, from a humble family, was inspired by the cult of the classical past then just gathering force in the beginnings of the Renaissance. He had himself proclaimed "tribune of liberty" and "liberator of the Holy Roman Republic." The people were won over quickly. The young man was successful at first also in defeating the opposition of the nobility, notably that of the Colonna, and was emboldened to undertake an extremely ambitious political program. He aimed to unite Italy in a federation under the leadership of Rome, *caput mundi*, and sent elegant Latin letters inviting the princes and republican governments of the peninsula to adhere. He dreamed even of re-establishing the Roman Empire and said in a speech delivered in the basilica of Saint John-in-Lateran: "We summon to our tribunal Pope Clement, and command him to reside in his diocese of Rome. We also summon the sacred college of Cardinals. We also summon the two pretenders, Charles of Bohemia and Louis of Bavaria, who style themselves [Holy Roman] Emperors. We likewise summon all the Electors of Germany to inform us on what pretense they have usurped the inalienable rights of the Roman people to elect the lawful sovereign of the empire."

Cola's pretensions were taken more seriously abroad than might have been expected—so awe-inspiring still were phrases like *Res Publica Romana* and *Senatus PopulusQue Romanus*—but his regime fell after a short time. His own vanity would have destroyed him even if the jealous barons had not done so. (Rather like Alexander the Great, he had taken to wearing outrageously sumptuous costumes.) The effect of the episode on Roman civic spirit was, however, enduring. Afterward there was always hidden sentiment against the pontiff's claims to temporal power in the city. Thus Lorenzo Valla, a celebrated Roman humanist of the mid-fifteenth century, secretly wrote a treatise disproving the authenticity of the Donation of Constantine, which was the theoretical basis of the popes' temporal power. Then, in the later fifteenth century, there arose in Rome a new intellectual movement of classical revival that might have had serious political results. Pomponius Laetus, who succeeded Valla as professor of eloquence in the Roman university, founded at his home on the Quirinal the Roman Academy, whose orientation was largely pagan and republican. Some ancient ceremonies were revived, and there was half-serious worship of the divine Genius of Rome. All members took pagan names, and Pomponius was given the title of Pontifex Maximus—officially belonging to the pope—as if *he* were the high priest of a state religion. Pope Paul II became seriously worried, on both theological and political grounds, fearing a *coup d'état* as much as heresy. He had twenty members of the academy arrested in 1468. Some of them were imprisoned in the Castel Sant' Angelo and put to the torture, and the pope himself sometimes came to take part in the interrogation. The academicians were released after having been very much frightened, and Pomponius was allowed to return to his chair of Latin eloquence in the university.

The academy was revived under the next pope, Sixtus IV, and the Emperor Frederick III gave it a *privilegium* (charter) in 1483. In that year the academy publicly celebrated for the first time the *Palilia*, anniversary of the founding of Rome. Pomponius and his friends were more cautious after their arrest and imprisonment, but it is unlikely that their ideas changed. The Roman Academy was an intellectual phenomenon of great local importance. Pomponius was immensely popular as a teacher, and it may be said that he formed the elite youth of Roman society for two generations. Many of his former students were mature men of means in the time of Pope Leo X, and Tomasso Inghirami, his successor in the chair of eloquence, was educating young men in the same tradition. Ideas of republican liberty were still cherished on the Campidoglio and among the elite of the native population. Expression of them had to be muffled in public, but they were doubtless discussed fervently in certain private circles.

Mature men in the period we are concerned with recalled vividly the powerful figure of Alexander VI, who had been pope from 1492 to 1503. Alexander is remembered popularly even today for his frank love affairs and for his venal maneuvers in favor of his extraordinary children, Lucrezia and Cesare Borgia. The times in which he ruled were crucial ones for Italy. He had become pope in the year that Lorenzo the Magnificent, peacemaker of the peninsula, died in Florence, and it fell his lot to be head of the Church during the first of the foreign invasions that were to ravage Italian Renaissance civilization. Charles VIII of France led a large army south in 1494, with the Kingdom of Naples as his destination. He entered Rome in triumph, though not precisely as a conqueror. The worried pope joined other states in the League of Venice, which forced Charles to leave the peninsula. A new French army under Louis XII came to Italy in 1499, and Spanish troops met it in battle there. The period of the Italian Wars had begun.

Despite his blatant faults, Alexander had been popular with many Romans because of his opposition to the French and because of his tolerance and sense of justice. (He had taken the trouble to go administer justice personally on the Campidoglio.) When he died, however, there was an outbreak of public joy of the sort that seemed nearly always to greet the ends of pontificates in the Renaissance. Pius III, the Piccolomini who succeeded Alexander, lived for only twenty-one days after his election. He was followed by Julius II, the first pope of our period and the real initiator of the Roman High Renaissance.

THE POPES

DURING THE Renaissance, as for long before and long afterward, the city of Rome and the Papal States were a principate ruled by the elected head of the Catholic Church. Pontificates are usually shorter than the reigns of kings, since they normally begin later in life, and the papal sovereigns of Rome seldom had the time to guide the city during even one whole generation. There were four popes during the quarter-century, 1503–27, with which we are concerned, and in order to understand the style of life and thought "at the top" during a period shorter than the Augustan Age we must look at the characters and interests of four different men. We shall consider their personalities in chronological order, giving most attention to that of Leo X, who symbolizes the whole age. Our emphasis will be on opinions, habits, and tastes rather than on specific actions and accomplishments, of which something more will be seen in other chapters.

Julius II, a member of the Ligurian family of Della Rovere, had owed his early preferment to the fact that Pope Sixtus IV, 1471–84, was his uncle. Julius's outstanding quality was his energy. This despite the fact that he was more than sixty years old when he became pope in 1503. He led vigorous campaigns to consolidate the territories of the Papal States and stood up to the king of France with fiery defiance. He was of a choleric character in his daily relations and is said once, when quite old, to have rushed out of his bedroom in the Vatican Palace to beat a guard who had been making noise nearby. The Romans feared him but admired his martial spirit and his efforts to drive the foreign "barbarians" out of Italy.

Julius was not considered to be a learned man, by the high humanistic standards of the time, and is not credited with any great personal discernment in matters of art. And yet he was one of the most successful patrons of art in European history. His success came from a second outstanding personal quality—that of vision. Like some better-remembered political leaders of old and recent history, he had a feeling for *la grandeur*, for the majesty of the state and the Church. It is to him that we owe the beginning of the construction of the new Saint Peter's, which he promoted with characteristic passion and energy. The project for his tomb, entrusted to Michelangelo, would, if it had been completed, have endowed Rome with the most grandiose monument in that genre since the time of the ancient emperors. On a smaller scale, but of no less august conception, is the decoration of the little Stanza della Segnatura, in the Vatican Palace, for which Julius commissioned Raphael. This little room contains allegorical frescoes representing the greatest men in the history of man's four major intellectual endeavors: Law, Poetry, Theology, and Philosophy. The last fresco, known as the *School of*

Athens, is often considered to be the finest expression in painting of the spirit and thought of the High Renaissance. The chief candidate as the finest such expression in architecture, Bramante's *Tempietto,* was also done in Rome during Julius's time. (Michelangelo's *David,* which might lay claim to the same distinction in sculpture, is also of the time but belongs to Florence.)

Julius was at the very least a fine judge of artists. He gave Michelangelo and Raphael their first important work in Rome; he entrusted the plans of Saint Peter's to Bramante. He also wisely built the Vatican's collection of antiquities (adding most notably the newly discovered statue called the *Laocoön*). He had as well a genuine esteem for literature, if little time for it. Toward the end of his life he asked the architect Bramante to explain to him Dante's *Divine Comedy.*

If Julius II is defined as a High Renaissance worthy by his actions, it is kinder to say of Leo X that he is important more by what he stood for than by what he did. What he stood for was the refinement of Florentine humanistic culture at its best. His election in 1513 caused perhaps the greatest outburst of joy Rome had ever shown on the advent of a new pontiff. The joy was based almost wholly on the fact that Leo was the son of Lorenzo the Magnificent. There could be no better recommendation in the Italy of 1513, which was in love with art and literature and which, having been cruelly tried by warfare since the death of Lorenzo, was now very much aware of his vanished accomplishments as a keeper of the peace. Giovanni was the second son of Lorenzo, having been born in 1475 in all the glory of Medici Florence at its peak. His father decided very early to prepare the boy for an ecclesiastical career. Giovanni was tonsured at age six and made a cardinal at thirteen.

Cardinal Giovanni dei Medici was in a position to receive a first class humanistic education, the best afforded by his time and one of the best of all times. We cannot be absolutely sure that he received it, but there are some indications that he did. His principal tutor was Angelo Poliziano, known in English as Politian, who was one of the glories of Italian vernacular literature and, as is less often remembered today, an extremely distinguished classical scholar. Politian's best Italian verse is in the light-hearted pastoral tradition, dear to the Renaissance (and execrated by modern sociological critics). He was the professor of Latin and Greek literature in Florence and lectured publicly on Homer, Vergil, Persius, Statius, Quintillian, and Suetonius. He is reported to have been the first Italian whose classical Greek was as good as that of the immigrant professors from Byzantium. He translated four books of the *Iliad* into Latin verse and did a great deal of valuable textual criticism.

The young man's second important tutor—there were other minor ones—was Bernardo da Bibbiena, whom he would one day make a cardinal. Bibbiena is remembered in Italian letters for the risqué and delightful comedy, *La Calandria*. He too was something of a prodigy at Latin studies and was well qualified to teach them, though he was only five years older than his pupil. His influence was to endure much longer than Politian's for he accompanied Giovanni to Rome and remained close to him in later life.

The intellectual and artistic life of Florence in the time of Lorenzo was illumined by the gentle star of the Platonic

Academy. This body had been founded by Marsilio Ficino under the protection of Cosimo the Elder dei Medici, Lorenzo's grandfather. Ficino was still its chief luminary. Among the others were Lorenzo himself, Politian, and the brilliant young Pico della Mirandola. The academy was dedicated to study of Plato and of the Neoplatonists. The presumed birthday of the philosopher was celebrated every year on November 7 with amiable discussions of one or more of the dialogues. Plato's philosophy was taken to be universally applicable, and Ficino liked to say that one could be neither a good citizen nor a good Christian without being a Platonist as well. It followed from this point of view that the Christian tradition did not have a monopoly on moral—much less aesthetic—truth. Christianity was seen, to be sure, as the best of religions but it was not above comparison with other systems, and it was not to be studied *in vacuo*. Florentine Neoplatonism had also a strong mystical content, centering around metaphorical visions of the universe as light, which is less interesting to twentieth-century minds.

It is not easy to deduce from the theory of the philosophy its applications in practical life. One of them was doubtless the balanced, historicist view of Christianity mentioned above. Another must have been the glorification of physical beauty, human and artistic, since the Platonic conception that earthly forms were imitations of ideal ones seems to have rebounded, in Renaissance Florence, to the glory of the former. And though divine love was shown as superior to profane, the latter gained from the relationship. There was also a view of all human endeavor as unified, with a consequent elevation in dignity of the activities of artisans. The beneficent influence of such ideas upon the flowering of art in Florence seems obvious enough, but like other subtle intellectual phenomena it would be hard to demonstrate in detail.

And thus while Roman intellectuals in the late *quattrocento* made a cult of Latinity and dreamed of the lost imperium, Florentine ones became Hellenists and admired the life of classical Athens. Giovanni dei Medici must have seen a great deal of members of the Platonic Academy at the Medici palace in Via Larga and in country villas near the city. In 1489, however, when he was only in his fourteenth year, he was sent by his father to the University of Pisa (in Florentine territory) to study civil and ecclesiastical law. These subjects must have seemed very dull compared to those he had heard discussed at home and doubtless continued to hear discussed among friends. In March, 1492, being considered of suitable age, he was ceremonially invested as a cardinal at the monastery of Fiesole.

Lorenzo the Magnificent died that same month, and two years later the Medici were expelled from Florence. For the next eighteen years, 1494–1512, the family were in exile, though far from destitute. Cardinal Giovanni did not get along well with Alexander VI, but under Julius II he was in high favor and lived handsomely in Rome in the town house now called Palazzo Madama. Pope Julius brought about a restoration of the Medici to rule in 1512. The cardinal, whose elder brother Piero had died, thus became unofficial ruler of his native city shortly before being elected pope.

Much has been written about the rather puzzling character of Leo X. He was chaste and had no violent passions except ambition for his family, an all too common weakness among Renaissance popes. He had an easygoing disposition and was inclined naturally toward kindness and generosity. Holding clerical austerity in small esteem, he was highly gregarious and greatly enjoyed social entertainments. He liked to dine in a large company and to take long hunting trips with a numerous, jolly entourage. In art, music, and literature, his taste was held to be exquisite, though poor eyesight prevented him from doing much reading on his own and from fully appreciating works of art that he could not get under his eyeglass. He had a strong sense of humor—not always extremely delicate— and was sometimes delightfully witty himself. His physical appearance was not at all attractive, for he was corpulent and his eyes bulged unbecomingly. Yet almost everyone had an excellent personal impression of him, and we can infer that he had an unusual amount of charm.

Leo's faults, apart from the nepotism mentioned above, were extensions of his easygoing character, which tended toward indolence and irresolution. He had many good intentions that were never carried through. This was true both in the realm of politics and in that of literary and artistic patronage. In political affairs, it is sure, the military weakness of the Papal States often tied his hands, and he was usually, except in nepotistic ventures, more sinned against than sinning. In cultural matters he might certainly, with the resources at hand, have accomplished much more. His famous generosity to musicians, artists, and literary men was often indiscriminate. And major projects, such as the improvement of the Roman university or *studio*, foundered when funds disappeared. For Leo X was an extremely poor manager of finances. Julius II, who knew the value of a *ducato*, had left the Vatican treasury in good shape, despite his costly wars. Leo left it nearly empty.

It is not surprising, in view of these faults, that Pope Leo's demonstrable achievements are fewer than those of Julius II. It is nevertheless true that he represented the High Renaissance far more brilliantly than his predecessor. Romans and Florentines alike were extremely proud of him.

The brief pontificate of Adrian VI, 1521–23, represents an interlude near the end of the Roman High Renaissance, and his character interests us because of its contrast with those of the other three popes of the period. Adrian was a Dutchman, born in Utrecht, though Italians, insensitive to national distinctions in the North, thought of him as a German. He was no stranger to courts and to power, having been the tutor of the young Emperor Charles V and having served that sovereign as a sort of regent in Spain, but he had not been corrupted by these experiences. His private life was austere and irreproachable. He was not fond of company or of entertainment. Though he was a brilliant Latinist and theologian, he had little active interest in belles-lettres or in art. The Ciceronian imitations of Roman *letterati* must, moreover, have seemed to him as ridiculous as they did to his countryman Erasmus, and his taste in architecture had presumably been formed by the Gothic churches of Northern Europe rather than by classical ruins or Italian Renaissance palaces.

Adrian set a personal example of thrift by reducing the Vatican household staff and by directing that he be served only simple dishes. He even talked of going to live elsewhere because the palace cost too much to keep up. The new pope was also bent upon moral reform, for he had heard much talk about the corruption of the Roman court and appreciated fully the importance of the Lutheran movement. He forbade the clergy to wear beards—considered momentarily to be a worldly affectation—and looked askance at rich apparel. He had, in sum, the best interests of religion and the Church at heart, but he was an alien in the society of early sixteenth-century Rome.

Clement VII, who became pope in 1524 at the age of forty-six, was in some ways a pale reflection of his cousin Leo X, with whom he had grown up. He was the son of Giuliano, the brother of Lorenzo the Magnificent who had been killed in the Pazzi Conspiracy of 1478, and the fact that Clement too was a Medici accounted for much of the general pleasure at his election. His character was, however, rather different from that of his cousin. He was less easygoing and less benevolent, and he had many more personal enemies. Before becoming pope, he had acquired a great deal of political experience, and he took a more energetic hand in affairs of state than Leo had done. He still was sometimes guilty of indecision, particularly in the events leading to the Sack of Rome. It was a different sort of indecision, more nervous and sporadic, but the effects were the same. They were, indeed, much worse because the dangers faced were greater.

Clement was less interested than Leo had been in art, letters, or music, and his table was less often a meeting place for brilliant society. He was much more careful with money and did not hand it out casually to musicians, writers, and artists. Yet, like Julius II, he knew the value of cultural achievements and realized that his own glory would be enhanced by them. He was in tune with the city and the age, though his political errors contributed to disasters that ended the age.

Such were the characters of the four men who stood at

the head of Roman society in the High Renaissance. We must now look at the peculiar structure of that society, at the conditions of its life, and at the activities, both admirable and unfortunate, which assure it a special place in cultural history.

POLITICS AND FOREIGN DANGERS

I F HIGH RENAISSANCE Rome was obsessed by history and classical revival, it was also intensely concerned with practical, contemporary politics. As in all capital cities, the fortunes of many citizens depended immediately upon local political decisions and arrangements, and here were powerful foreign political pressures which were felt much more keenly than in Paris or London.

The governmental structure of the Eternal City was unique. There existed, as we have seen, a republican municipal government formally analogous to those of genuine *comuni* and city-states. It was established on the glorious Campidoglio, the Capitoline Hill of ancient times. This government included as principal officers a single senator, three *conservatori*, and one *caporione* for each *rione*, or district, of the city. It had never been really sovereign—except for the quixotic moment with Cola di Rienzo—though its ambitions were still alive and it had ceremonial functions that were carried out in grand style. Rome was in fact ruled by an almost absolute monarch, the pope. Like that of the Holy Roman Empire, this monarchy was elective rather than hereditary. The supreme pontiff was chosen by the College of Cardinals, each of whose members had been appointed by a previous pope. Some men said that the cardinals also had the right to approve or disapprove the pontiff's most important actions, but that right was not well defined. During an interregnum between the death of one pope and the election of another, the College of Cardinals was formally responsible for governing the city and the Church. The pontifical administration was very large indeed, with a number of special commissions and bureaus dealing with both spiritual and temporal matters. In its complexity it bore comparison with the imperial administration of ancient Rome. None of the pontifical officers, of course, were elected by the population. The conferring of prestigious and lucrative offices was a great source of power, and sometimes of funds, for a new pope.

This mixture of temporal and spiritual affairs must seem to us unhealthy, and by the nineteenth century, Italians were ready to take away the pope's temporal power. But if Romans in the Renaissance resented the prevalence of outsiders in positions of authority, they took pride in the unique status of their city. The pope in their eyes was a link with the glorious imperial past. Though the titles of *Caesar* and *Imperator* were now conferred by the seven German electors instead of the *Senatus PopulusQue Romanus,* the ruler of their city retained one of the titles of the ancient emperors, that of Pontifex Maximus. The pope's spiritual power seemed to add to their own temporal status. They felt themselves to be at the center of Christendom and of European culture. Like many Romans of today, they considered the pope and the resident cardinals to be their personal property.

If Romans had had little recent experience at governing themselves, they knew all about political intrigue and conflict. The basic rivalry between the Orsini and Colonna families, centuries old and still smacking of the Guelf-Ghibelline wars of the Middle Ages, divided most of the old native families into two camps on critical occasions. It was a rare political event that pleased both sides. As for the great numbers of foreigners in the city, many of them had come to Rome almost as delegates go to the United Nations—in order to advance the interests of their homelands. In these special Roman conditions a nervous political life was assured.

The greatest of all political events was of course the election of a new pope. Rome was in a state of fever during interregna. Many people were sincerely concerned for the future of the Church; many others were anxious about their jobs or chances for advancement. Such periods were longer than they are now. It took some time for absent cardinals to get to Rome, and there were also political deadlocks of some duration that would be unthinkable today. Betters in the city amused themselves by wagering on the result of the conclave, and satirists grew bold, particularly in attacking the pope who had just died. The Campidoglio government usually seized the occasion to try to wring political concessions from the cardinals governing the city. Crowds gathered in front of the Vatican Palace (not yet in Bernini's fine baroque piazza), while inside the cardinals, sitting in much discomfort, deliberated and voted as many times as necessary. When the result was announced, the population burst into expressions of joy or anger. We shall see something of the conclaves of 1521 and 1524 in the Epilogue.

The Roman public also followed with enormous interest less important developments within the *Curia* and College of Cardinals. Many small men's fortunes depended upon those of one particular prince of the Church, and ecclesiastical politics were inseparable from the economic life of the city. Everyone wished to know what was said and done at formal consistories, which cardinals seemed to have the pope's ear, and so on. Clerical gossips found eager listeners.

Political and military events on an international scale had particularly severe repercussions in Rome, both because the city was more dependent than others on foreign good will and because it counted among its residents many men who owed allegiance to foreign powers. The time was not one of peace and security. A glance at the general Italian and European political scenes in the early sixteenth century shows why the popes and their Roman subjects were often in states of anxiety.

The most powerful states in Western Europe were France, Spain, the Holy Roman Empire, and England. France was a remarkably unified nation for the period, and it had a large and energetic population. Spain was in a period of national expansion and glory with dependencies in Europe and America. The Empire had great resources but was loosely constructed. (In 1519 Spain and the Empire were united under the power of Charles V.) England was vigorous and a thorn in the side of France, though still relatively small in population and economic power. The kings of France and Spain and the emperor had already demonstrated territorial ambitions in Italy, which was in some ways, if not all, the richest country of the Continent. The pontificate of Leo X came a bit before midway in the Italian Wars, 1494–1559, during which foreign armies fought on the peninsula.

Italy was not a nation and would not be one for more than three hundred more years. The more or less democratic and civic-minded city-states of the late Middle Ages and early Renaissance were mostly declining, and democracy as a political ideal was definitely in retreat. Milan, in the north, bore the brunt of foreign cupidity and was captured several times by French, Spanish, or German troops. Florence, which we like to think of as the prototype of the democratic *comune*, came back under Medici rule in 1512, after a period of republican freedom. It was a traditional ally of France, but the Medici had been restored by Spanish troops. Siena, between Florence and Rome, maintained a precarious independence. Once proud Genoa was weak and would soon lose its freedom. Venice, on the other hand, remained strong and ambitious and would manage to preserve its independence through all the dangers of two and one-half more centuries. The south of Italy, which had scarcely known city-states, was mostly included in the Kingdom of Naples, under Spanish rule since 1504. The Papal States occupied the center of the fragmented peninsula.

One must add to the facts of this European and Italian situation the frightening proximity of Ottoman Turkey, not a part of Christendom but present in Europe and the Mediterranean. Christian populations had been overrun, and Central Europe and the shores of the Mediterranean waited in fear of more Turkish expansion. Mohammedan pirates terrorized maritime commerce and coastal villages.

The popes' responsibilities in foreign affairs were heavy and often conflicting. All four men in our period were anxious to get Christian powers to unite in a crusade against the Turks. Efforts in this direction were an utter failure; the various monarchs were happy to approve the idea in principle but not ready to suspend their rivalries. Julius, Leo, and Clement also felt deeply a duty toward Italy, a duty to keep foreign domination in the peninsula at a minimum (though not to promote national unity). As temporal sovereigns, however, the pontiffs considered too that they must defend and, if possible, enlarge, the territories of the Papal States. That led them into alliances with some Christian powers against others and much diminished their spiritual prestige. The two Medici, moreover, had to look out for the interests of their personal principate of Florence. Far worse, they felt obliged to advance political ambitions of their relatives. When Leo X had papal armies take the Dukedom of Urbino away from its rightful prince so that it might be given to his worthless nephew Lorenzo dei Medici, his moral stature fell very low. How, after that, could he expect Francis I and Charles V to listen to his pleas for peace among Christian nations? In its effects nepotism was perhaps the worst fault of Renaissance popes.

Militarily the Papal States were a distinctly minor power, and spiritual authority was of little use in the situations of war. Both Julius II and Clement VII found that excommunication was an inefficient weapon against invaders. From our vantage point it may seem that the popes would have been wise to remain neutral in all conflicts between Christian states, but that would in practice have been almost impossible. Rome and the Vatican court contained fervent advocates of all national interests (except of the Turks), as well as of countless private ones. In Pope Leo's time Giuliano and Lorenzo dei Medici were warm friends of France, as were also a few cardinals and the powerful local faction led by the Orsini family. Cousin Giulio dei Medici (later Clement VII), many other cardinals, and the Colonna faction liked Spain and the Empire. The many Florentines at the Vatican remembered the interests of their city and of the Medici family. Venice also had insistent agents. It is hard to guess the relative strength of "Italians," that is, of men devoted to the welfare of the whole peninsula. The greatest of them, Niccolo Machiavelli, was away in Florence, more or less out of favor with the Medici family though eager to give advice.

There is no space here to give a systematic history of the papacy's involvement in international affairs during the High Renaissance, nor for our purposes would the fruits of such an enterprise be commensurate with its difficulty and tediousness. We may, however, gain an idea of the whole by looking at a few major military and political events during the pontificate of Leo X, with particular attention to their immediate repercussions in the city of Rome. (Later, in the Epilogue, we shall have occasion to see the events leading immediately to the Sack of Rome.) Repercussions were delayed by the slowness of travel and transport. Indeed, it was impossible for anyone to be sure that he was posted on the latest developments. Florence was two days away; it took many days to receive a message from Spain, France, or Germany. Rumors thrived far more than in our own day; one could hear of battles that had never occurred, of victories that had been defeats. Military preparations and movements were slower too, however, and this in some way compensated for the weakness of communication. To cite the most poignant contemporary example, it took the king of France or the emperor a great while to raise an army and prepare to move into Italy, and there was time for the peninsula to prepare.

Julius II had warred against France, and, on Pope Leo's accession, relations between the Holy See and King Louis XII were virtually broken. In May, 1512, a new French army entered Italy, hoping to recapture Milan, and an allied Venetian army approached Milan from the other direction. On June 6, at the Lombard town of Novara, the French were badly beaten by the Swiss mercenaries of the Sforza Duke of Milan. News of the battle reached Rome on June 10—four days later. Pro-Spanish and pro-Imperial parties of the city celebrated publicly. Cardinal Schinner, fierce partisan of the emperor, had the bells of his Roman church rung. The pontiff was gratified but did not wish a complete humiliation of France. He moved to receive back into good standing some quasi-heretic cardinals who had defied Julius by sitting in a church council at Pisa sponsored by King Louis. The guilty prelates were allowed to enter Rome at night, without the insignia of their rank. On June 27 they had to ask forgiveness publicly in the presence of the pope and cardinals in consistory. According to Vatican diarist Paride dei Grassi, so many people had come to the palace to witness this humiliation that they filled the stairways and corridors. There was even fear that some of the floors might collapse.

At the beginning of 1515, Louis XII was succeeded as king of France by the young Francis I, a monarch of vast energy whose interest in Italy was to be obsessive and enduring. In the early summer he crossed the Alps with a large army, determined to take back Milan and more. Venice was again France's partner. The pope was allied with the emperor, the Duke of Milan, and the Spanish viceroy of Naples against the invaders, although he had instructed his nephew Lorenzo, captain of the papal armies, to enter the fray only if there seemed to be no risk. On September 13–14, at Marignan, the French won a brilliant victory over Swiss mercenaries, giving those proud professionals the greatest humiliation of their history. The first news, received in Rome on September 16, reported a Swiss victory and caused widespread rejoicing among Spaniards, Imperials, and most officers of the Church. Cardinal Bibbiena ordered a public celebration, but the pope, fortunately, did not show his hand quite so clearly. The next morning he was awakened to receive the Venetian ambassador, who was delighted to bring the true news of a French victory, saying hypocritically: "Holy Father, following the example of Christ I want to repay evil with good. Yesterday Your Holiness gave me some news that was both bad and false; today, on the contrary, I bring you some that is both good and true—the Swiss are defeated."

The poor pontiff, losing his normal urbane composure, exclaimed in Latin: *"Quid ergo erit de nobis, et quid de vobis?"* ("What, then, will become of us, and of you too?"). The Venetian said joyfully that he had no worries at all since his homeland was an ally of France and (with great malice) that the Holy Father had nothing to fear either from a Christian king.

Most of the Roman court were very much frightened, expecting a French invasion of the Papal States and of Rome itself. The pope resolved upon the extreme course of going to meet Francis personally in Bologna. This despite the shocked opinion of advisers that a pope would demean himself by seeking out a sovereign. There were, however, better arguments against having Francis visit Rome in the company of his army. After a long and difficult journey, with an enormous entourage, Leo reached Florence at the end of November. The Florentines' grand reception of him in his first visit as pope rivaled the greatest ceremonial displays of Rome. In early December he arrived in Bologna, where the anti-Florentine inhabitants greeted him with small affection. The ceremonial preparations for the meeting of the two sovereigns were unbelievably complex, and disputes arose among officers of protocol. Francis arrived a few days after Leo, and the conferences were begun, with much mutual flattery and show of affection. The young French king, who had the grace of a perfect Renaissance courtier, behaved with great deference toward the pontiff. So also did his officers, who had not felt scruples on fighting against Church armies. On one occasion a number of them emotionally confessed to having sinned against Julius II and asked Leo's pardon. It was quickly given. The Frenchmen then kissed his foot with such passion that, according to an observer, it was almost "eaten up."

The two sovereigns agreed more or less amicably on various questions. Francis received Parma and Modena but apparently was dissuaded from marching on south. Some questions concerning the Church in France were settled to the satisfaction of monarch and pope (though not, it developed, to that of the French clergy). No formal alliance was concluded. The concrete agreements of the meeting were not announced. Talk in public was all about

the desirability of establishing peace among Christian nations and forming a league against the Turks.

The Pope and his court returned to Rome only on February 28, 1516. He had tarried on the way back in Florence,
where his brother Giuliano lay dying. The gentle Giuliano
had tried to dissuade his brother from the conquest of the
Dukedom of Urbino for their nephew Lorenzo. Both broth-
ers had received hospitality there during their exile from
Florence. The dowager Duchess Elisabetta, great lady of
Castiglione's *The Courtier*, came to Rome in person to plead
the case of the rightful duke, Francesco Maria della Rovere.
Her entreaties availed nothing. The shameful enterprise
was undertaken, and, after a costly and inglorious military campaign, victory was celebrated at Rome in June.

In April of 1516 a small local event occurred that caused
great alarm in Rome and throws light for us on one of the
pope's main obsessions, his fear of the Turks. While he
was staying at Città Lavinia, a lovely pastoral spot near
the mouth of the Tiber, a ship containing Mohammedan
pirates—Turkish, Arab, or nondescript—arrived on the
coast. The pirates raided nearby towns and carried off a
number of persons as prisoners. It was rumored that their
intention had been to seize the pope himself. He fled in
haste to Rome, where there was great shock. What if the
head of the Church had been taken as a prisoner to Constantinople?

The most important series of events of the whole period
began on October 31, 1517, when Martin Luther posted his
Ninety-five Theses on the cathedral door at Wittenberg.
We shall, however, give these events little attention because most of them took place in Northern Europe and
tell us little about life in the city of Rome. The reactions

of the pope and *Curia* to Luther's early actions were remarkably slow and restrained. The anti-Roman character of the new movement was evident very early, though the reformer continued for some time to express confidence in the Pope's personal character. But at the Vatican the affair must have seemed at first like a minor—and rather interesting—theological controversy, a new dispute between Augustinians and Dominicans.

The sale of indulgences, which Leo had authorized in 1515 to raise funds for the construction of the new Saint Peter's, appeared to worldly Romans a small matter to raise such a fuss over. During 1518 the pope tried to bring Luther to heel through monastic discipline and diplomatic pressure on the emperor. But Luther stuck to his ideas and turned out an astonishing quantity of polemical writings. He was protected by his prince, Frederick, Elector of Saxony. In March, 1519, Leo sent him a kindly worded letter inviting him to come to Rome to retract his errors. The invitation was not accepted, and an irrevocable break came in 1520. After four consistories in late May and early June, the College of Cardinals approved the papal bull *Exsurge Domine*, which, without mentioning Luther's name, condemned forty-one of his assertions and prohibited everyone, on pain of excommunication, from supporting them. Shortly afterward some of Luther's writings were burned publicly at the Agone (today's Piazza Navona) in a ceremony that gave most Romans their first realization of the seriousness of the crisis. On December 10, Luther reciprocated the gesture by burning the bull and other documents publicly at Wittenberg.

There were other events in Germany that interested contemporary Romans more than the early activities of Luther. The Emperor Maximilian I died suddenly on January 12, 1519. He had recently tried unsuccessfully to pick his heir by having his young grandson, King Charles I of Spain, designated "King of the Romans," Imperial equivalent of the British Prince of Wales, Pope Leo had resisted this project and was not enthusiastic, either, about the Imperial ambitions of Francis I, an equally powerful monarch. During the campaigns for election after Maximilian's death, the pontiff held out hope of support to both the French and the Spanish sovereigns while really hoping for the choice of the minor prince Frederick of Saxony. (Frederick would not have been dangerous and, in return for papal support, might have been expected to suppress Martin Luther. The history of Europe would have been different.) But Charles of Spain was chosen on June 28. Thus was created a concentration of power in one man's hands such as Europe had not known since Charlemagne and would not know again until the time of Napoleon. Charles controlled Spain, the Empire, the Kingdom of Naples, and most of the Low Countries. He wanted still more, and only the tenacious opposition of Francis I was to prevent him from becoming the master of the Continent.

The news of Charles's election reached Rome on July 5. The Spaniards in town and the local Colonna faction celebrated wildly in the streets, shouting, *"Impero e Spagna."* Several hundred armed men trooped around for two evenings, stopping in at friendly palaces for refreshment. The French and the Orsini party were abject. The pontiff himself was in a very low mood; a few days after the news had arrived, he asked the Venetian ambassador: "What must

I do if the Hapsburg comes to Italy now? All of Germany would help him." But a flattering and elegant letter of congratulation was sent to the new Charles V.

In all the lively local and international political activity of Rome during the period, nothing was accomplished that can bear comparison with the political achievements of the Age of Augustus. The confusedly democratic aspirations of the Campidoglio government came to naught. The popes failed, first, to promote peace in Europe, second, to protect Italy from foreign domination, and third, to preserve the unity of the Western Christian church. And we must add to these failures the fact that political life in Rome, however passionate and intense, had few of the noble and uplifting qualities that distinguished civic participation in the Athens of Pericles or in Florence at its best periods. It was not only that everyone knew the citizenry could not determine the policies of the government; a very large proportion of the population was in fact more concerned with the interests of foreign powers than with those of the city in which they were residing. Party lines were usually along the lines of foreign allegiance and local family feuds rather than along those of ideological differences. It is not in Rome that the great Renaissance historian Jacob Burckhardt found "the state as a work of art," and it is not for its politics that the Roman High Renaissance merits a place among the great ages of western civilization.

COSMOPOLIS AND BOOM TOWN

A MAN FAMILIAR with the Rome of today would have much difficulty recognizing the city of 1513. He would be disoriented less, perhaps, by the lack of recent buildings than by the presence of countless medieval structures now gone and by the absence of all the baroque constructions—churches, fountains, and palaces—that give the city its "old-fashioned" character in the twentieth century. Most of the 1513 buildings were medieval in origin (if often constructed with materials gleaned from ancient ruins). There were many plain, massive brick structures of undistinguished quality. Few of these survive today, and to get an idea of what central Rome must have looked like, one must visit other Italian cities in which whole medieval quarters have been preserved. The general effect of such architecture was, however, somewhat superior in the Eternal City, for its citizens had often decorated the façades of dull buildings with Corinthian columns or fragments of sculpture taken from ancient ruins.

The classical ruins we know now were present, but not always in a recognizable form. Tall constructions like the

Colosseum, the Castel Sant' Angelo, and Trajan's Column stood out clearly from a distance though there might be medieval slums built right on to them, but the Pantheon, not particularly visible today from afar, was probably even better camouflaged then. The forums were grown up in vegetation (grazed on by cattle or goats) and cluttered with temporary structures. Many columns now standing were then lying on the ground. Medieval cities tended to be extremely crowded, and there were indeed crowded quarters in Rome, but the city was unique demographically in that it held fewer than sixty thousand people in an area that had once contained over one million. There must have been vast open spaces and other wide areas covered with undistinguished ruins that have long since been cleared away.

There were two main centers of activity in the city: the Campidoglio and the Vatican. The Campidoglio had already been for a long time the city's civic center, but its magnificent architectural ensemble designed by Michelangelo was still a number of years in the future, and the hill boasted only two mediocre medieval *palazzi* and the church of Aracoeli. Even here, animals were sometimes allowed to graze. The business center of the medieval city, with a large open-air market, clustered at the foot of the Campidoglio. The Vatican, across the Tiber, lay next to a quarter or suburb called "Leonine"—not in honor of our pontiff but after his ninth-century predecessor Leo IV. This area was to build up a great deal during the sixteenth century, as were several other sections along both sides of the Tiber. The Vatican and Saint Peter's continued to be, however, more or less on the edge of town in comparison with the Campidoglio, though they were busy with many activ-

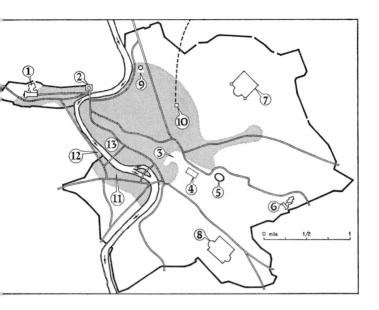

Rome *circa* 1520 with ancient Aurelian walls and principal streets. Densely populated areas are indicated by shading.

1. Saint Peter's and the Vatican Palace
2. Castel Sant' Angelo
3. Campidoglio
4. Ancient forums
5. Colosseum
6. St. John-in-Lateran Palace
7. Baths of Diocletian
8. Baths of Caracalla
9. Mausoleum of Augustus
10. Trevi Fountain, served by *Acqua Vergine* Aqueduct
11. Trastevere quarter
12. Villa Suburbana of Agostino Chigi
13. Farnese Palace

ities. At the other end of town were Saint John-in-Lateran and its palace, which had been the center of ecclesiastical government before the Avignonese exile. This area was now rather quiet and considered to be truly on the periphery of Rome. Trastevere, across the Tiber like the Vatican, was also a bit distant from the center, but it had enjoyed a bustling life through the Middle Ages.

Rome was to be transformed by growth and new construction in the sixteenth and early seventeenth centuries. The city was at the beginning of a period of boom, and its quality as a boom town contrasted most strangely to its proud status as the most venerated ancient city of Western Europe. One was immersed in tradition in Rome, but also immersed in novelty and bustle, and the city must have seemed to thoughtful visitors to be suffering from a sort of split personality.

This sixteenth-century boom had two principal causes: greater spending by a more prosperous Church, and an increased flow of humanistic tourists, pilgrims, and well-to-do immigrants. As in imperial times, the wealth of the city came principally from elsewhere. Rome was an international city supported by the Catholic and humanistic world. With its new population, it was rapidly becoming a modern cosmopolis, comparable in demographic diversity to the Alexandria, Rome, and Constantinople of certain periods in antiquity.

A census of the city done in 1526–27, called a *Descriptio urbis*, gives us some idea of the composition of the population in the early part of the century. The census was done by households (*fuochi*, or, literally, torches), with the householder's name and the number of people living with him being noted. Sometimes there is also information about the origin and occupation of the householder. The permanent population works out as 53,897 inhabitants—about the same as Florence but considerably fewer than were living in Milan and Naples. If the 3,000-odd names of householders with their origins indicated are a fair sample, only 17 per cent of the inhabitants were Roman by origin. Sixty-three per cent were from other parts of Italy, principally Tuscany and Lombardy, and 20 per cent were non-Italians. It is hard to believe that these indications are exact, but one cannot doubt that the population of Rome was a cosmopolitan one with the Tuscan and northern Italian elements predominant.

The old native Romans doubtless viewed the influx of new people with conflicting emotions. On the one hand, they did not relish being outnumbered in their own city, and they did not like to see the old customs disregarded or derided. Some of the newcomers, notably the Florentines, could be supercilious and arrogant in their relations with the natives. Romans might appear to them as a sleepy and rather old-fashioned people. A Florentine, if he had had our chronological vocabularies and categories to work with, might have said that his city was modern, while Rome was no longer classical and, not having reached modernity, was essentially medieval. Patriotic Romans would have replied that the classical tradition had never been broken in their city and that being modern elsewhere was merely a matter of rediscovering what Romans had never lost.

On the other hand, many of the new people brought money with them, and the boom meant profits at least for landowners and merchants. There could be no objection to increased local profits, even if they were largely offset by the rise in cost of living. Moreover, the growth of population and the building projects rebounded to the glory of the Eternal City. One could not stand in the way of progress, the local boosters must have thought. But this progress was not exactly along the lines old Romans would have mapped out. If they could have had their wishes, the pope would have been nearly always a Roman (provided he did not belong to a family feuding with theirs) and the civic government, still termed the *SPQR*, would have had far greater powers and prestige. Latin—which could be learned properly only in Rome—would have been the written language for literature, and the Roman dialect of Italian would have been the vehicle of everyday conversation. Newcomers to the city would have had to accept assimilation and would have sought Roman citizenship humbly, once they became worthy. This is how the old Romans would have liked to see things done. But they were not in control of the situation, and their power diminished along with their proportion of the population. Similar frustrations have been endured by old settlers in American boom towns.

Native Romans of the time are, paradoxically, less well known to us than many outlanders, for they were not usually important in the Vatican or in literary circles. There was one, however, who wrote a great deal and whose character and opinions we know very well. This was Marc Antonio Altieri, a member of the second rank of Roman nobility and an important figure in the Campidoglio government. He had been born in 1450, probably in his family's palace near the present Gesù church. He had studied in his youth under Pomponius Laetus, at the *studio*, and had acquired from him, besides a good classical education, a fierce local patriotism and partly repressed republican and anti-clerical opinions. In 1511 Altieri was a main orator at a great meeting of the nobles on the Campidoglio called to end old feuds. He evoked the past glories of Rome and her more recent misfortunes. Now, because of internal disorders, he said, the city was "given as a prey to the whole world." Listeners were so carried away that they decided to suspend some feuds, if not all. At another Campidoglio meeting of about the same time, when it was rumored that Pope Julius II was dying, Altieri is said by the historian Paolo Giovio to have urged his fellow Romans to surround the imminent conclave and force the cardinals to grant large political concessions to the city. He was also one of the proudest municipal officials at the festivities for the granting of citizenship to Lorenzo and Giuliano dei Medici in 1513, and he wrote one of the fullest accounts of the proceedings.

Altieri left in manuscript two ambitious literary works, both published in the nineteenth century. *Li Nuptiali*, a rather long treatise in dialogue form, concerns itself mainly with old Roman marriage customs but also with other matters of personal interest to the author. *L'Amorosa* is a philosophical tale. Altieri composed as well an elaborate will that is more than a business document. In it he urged that the anniversary of Rome's founding, the *Natale di Roma*, be celebrated on the Campidoglio every year with lectures on segments of the city's history. Altieri was a cultivated and sincere local patriot who thought of himself as a defender of his class and way of life.

The natives did not see all outlanders in the same light. Italians from other parts of the peninsula, while sometimes resented, did not seem entirely foreign, and Romans could at least converse with them without too much difficulty (provided that both parties had a minimum of education or cosmopolitan experience, since a peasant from the Piedmont would have had much trouble making himself understood to a yokel from the Roman countryside). Tuscans and Lombards were now to be found at virtually all levels of society, and the native attitude toward them must have varied in relation to their individual characters and degree of success in local business or politics.

The wealthiest and most prominent private citizen in Rome was in fact a Tuscan immigrant. He was not, however, a Florentine and had not come in the train of the Medici pope. Agostino Chigi was a Sienese banker who had taken over a bank in the busy Via dei Banchi. In the past the Eternal City had not been a major financial and commercial center to compare with Florence or Venice, but Chigi became one of the wealthiest men in Europe. Much of his power came from close financial relations with the Vatican as a creditor and a sort of treasurer. His bank had a number of branches abroad, and the sultan of Turkey is supposed to have known him as "the great Christian merchant."

Like the best of the early Medici, Chigi combined the ability to make money with genuine artistic taste and humanistic interests. He was a close friend of Raphael, perhaps that artist's closest friend. He founded a printing house that issued an edition of the Greek poet Pindar in 1515. He built a beautiful villa that survives in good condition as the Villa Farnesina in today's Via della Lungara. In Chigi's time it was called "La Suburbana" because it was located on a still rural stretch of the right bank of the Tiber between Saint Peter's and Trastevere. Baldassare

Peruzzi, who went on to become the architect of Saint Peter's, was mainly responsible for the design. Raphael decorated walls with frescoes showing mythological and allegorical scenes. In his magnificent villa Chigi gave lavish entertainments that mixed artistic excellence with nouveau riche ostentation. Pope Leo came to lunch in the company of cardinals several times. On one such occasion, on April 30, 1518, the stables had been lined with silk to make them fit dining rooms. At the end of that lunch, attended by many notables, a number of silver plates and vessels were discovered to be missing, but the generous banker said nothing. After at least one other luncheon he had his servants throw the dirty dishes in the river—where they were, however, caught by a submerged net. At still another banquet distinguished guests received silverware engraved with their coats of arms, and an attempt was made to serve them with dishes from their own regions. Such magnificence was much talked about and a source of pride in the city. When Chigi died in 1520, he received a funeral rivalling in grandeur that of a pope.

It was the Spaniards who probably constituted the largest truly foreign colony in Rome. Romans could talk to Spaniards, after a fashion, as Italians and Spanish-speaking people can communicate even today on an elementary level. Some old Spanish settlers, who had come in the time of the Borgia Pope Alexander VI, were more or less assimilated and spoke a sort of Italian. Some common people, like the fictional character La Loçana andaluza, whom we shall meet a little later, could be without national presumption and fit in well among people of their own class. Spaniards who had a connection with their national government or army were, however, detested and feared. They were known for their arrogance—to the point that the word *spagnuolo* was sometimes a synonym for that quality.

Frenchmen, worst enemies of the Spaniards, were rarer in Rome, particularly as settled immigrants. We have, however, the diary of an anonymous, nearly assimilated Frenchman who recorded his experiences from 1509 to 1540. This manuscript work, still unpublished but studied by the French historian Louis Madelin, gives a host of details on historical events and also on practical life in the city. The author was probably a cleric who had come to Rome with a high French church official and had settled down there with some sort of employment at the Vatican. He owned a vineyard and talks a great deal about the weather and its effects on the vines. Though he shows much interest in the French royal family, his political allegiance is to the papacy. When Julius II is the bitter enemy of France, he reports the pope's actions against his native land and permits himself only (on two occasions) the cautious remark *"Je ne sçay que ce sera"*—"I don't know how that will work out." He takes a special interest in the foundation of the French church in Rome, Saint-Louis des Français, but he is basically a first-generation Roman. He enjoys going to all grand public ceremonies and also to less edifying spectacles such as executions. He talks a great deal about building going on in the city, about business conditions, and, especially in the later years, about appointments and politics in the College of Cardinals. Local events are more important to him than international ones; this cleric living in Rome during the first decades of the sixteenth century does not mention the Lutheran movement.

Rome had a surprisingly large colony of Germans. One

has the impression that there was less resentment toward them than toward the Spaniards, and even the French. They did not evoke the same sort of foreign threat. Germany was not a unified nation, and its inhabitants did not yet have the reputation for fierce warfare that they would hold after the Sack of Rome in 1527—and which they have acquired again in our times. The Holy Roman Empire, mainly German, did not breed the same kind of chauvinism as the more integrated monarchies of France and Spain. If anything, their "imperial" heritage may have made Germans feel a kinship with Romans rather than a superiority over them. The Germans in Rome, if not students and scholars, were often small business people who learned Italian and fitted into local society better than most Frenchmen and Spaniards. The worst qualities popularly attributed to Germans were gluttony and drunkenness.

The English were a small colony, and one reads comparatively little about them in contemporary documents. They were no longer so exotic as in the sixth century, when Pope Gregory the Great, seeing handsome English boys who had been brought to Rome, said they were "not Angles but Angels" (*non angli sed angeli*), but were nevertheless rather few. Their small number was partly a reflection of the fact that England was still, by its population, in the second rank of European nations and partly a result of its distance from Rome. Henry VIII—though a strong and most ambitious monarch highly concerned with ecclesiastical politics—was not in a position to intervene materially in peninsular affairs.

The most distinct and most alienated of the minorities in Rome were the Jews, of whom the *Descriptio* indicated a resident population of 1,750 persons. Jews had traditionally received better treatment at the hands of the Vicar of Christ than from secular Christian princes, and Rome had long been a favorite city for their residence. Many of those in the city at the beginning of the century had been expelled from Spain, which was already less tolerant than the rest of Western Europe in various things. Later, in the Counter-Reformation, a Roman ghetto would be established on the example of the one in Venice. In Pope Leo's time most Jews lived in the center near the Campidoglio, but there were no systematic restrictions on their movements. The French pilgrim Jacques Le Saige (of whom we shall see more shortly) was shocked in 1519 by the size and freedom of the Jewish population: "I was quite astonished to see so many Jews. When they go through the town they have a red garter on their breasts so that one can recognize them. . . . I saw them observe the holiday on Saturday, and quite near there the Christians were working. I heard it said that these cursed Jews work in their closed houses on Sunday. They pay a large tribute to the Pope. That is why no one dares do anything to them, for it would be dangerous."

When Pope Leo rode to the Lateran to take ceremonial possession of that palace at the beginning of his pontificate, he paused along the way to receive the congratulations of the Jewish community. Following a traditional ritual, they offered him a copy of their Law, which he examined and then let fall, saying, *"Confirmamus sed non consentimus."* With this consecrated phrase he recognized their limited civic rights without giving any approval to their religion. The Jews in Rome were engaged mainly in commerce. They could not hold civic or political offices—except by being baptized—though they were sometimes accepted into

Christian society on an informal basis. If their lives and property were relatively safe, they had to bear countless humiliations. Two scenes of Aretino's play *La Cortigiana* are so evocative of what it was like to be a Jew in the capital of Christendom that they merit being reproduced in full. The rascal Rosso, seeking new clothes for a disguise, meets a Jewish peddler in the street:

Jew: Old iron! Old iron!

Rosso: Come here, Jew.

Jew: What do you command?

Rosso: What kind of cloak is that?

Jew: It used to belong to Cavalier Brandino. And such cloth!

Rosso: What is it worth?

Jew: Try it on and then we'll talk about the price.

Rosso: That's a good idea.

Jew: Take your cape off first. Put your arm in here; May I never see the Messiah if it doesn't seem made for you! What a fashionable cloak!

Rosso: Tell me the truth.

Jew: May God not take me to the synagogue on the sabbath if it doesn't fit you perfectly!

Rosso: Now let's get to the price, and if you really make me a good deal I will buy also that friar's hood for a brother of mine who is in Aracoeli.

Jew: If you take this hood too I'll make you a real bargain, and, by the way, it belonged to the Most Reverend Aracoeli In Minoribus.

Rosso: So much the better. But because my brother is difficult for his clothes, I want to see it on your back and then we shall make a deal.

Jew: I am glad to put it on, so that you can spend your farthings with assurance.

Rosso: You dropped the cord. Now put on the scapular. It is certainly a fine garment!

Jew: And such cloth!

Rosso: You certainly seem to be a fine fellow; I've thought of a good idea for you.

Jew: Damn!

Rosso: I want you to become a Christian.

Jew: You want to argue. You believe in God and I believe in God. If you want to buy that's one thing, and if you want to argue that's another.

Rosso: It's a sin to do you a favor. Who said anything about your soul? The soul's the least important thing.

Jew: Take off my cloak.

Rosso: Listen to me. I want you to become a Christian for three reasons.

Jew: Take it off, I say!

Rosso: Listen, Beast. If you become a Christian, in the first place, the day you are baptized you will receive a bowl full of coins and then all of Rome will come to see you crowned with olive, which is a fine thing.

Jew: You are amusing yourself.

Rosso: Another thing is that you will eat pork.

Jew: I care little about that.

Rosso: Little? If you tasted *pane unto* [bread fried in lard], you would deny a hundred Messiahs for the love of it. Oh what a melody is *pane unto* around the fire, with a jug between the legs, and greasing the bread and eating and drinking!

Jew: Please, give me my cloak because I have things to do.

48

Rosso: The last is that you will not wear the sign on your breast.

Jew: What does that matter?

Rosso: It matters, because the Spaniards would like to crucify you for such a sign.

Jew: Why crucify me?

Rosso: Because you seem to be one of them when you wear it.

Jew: But there's a difference between us and them.

Rosso: But there's not any difference at all if you wear it. And then if you don't wear the sign of a Jew anymore, the boys will not pelt you all day long with oranges and melon rinds. . . . And so, become a Christian, become a Christian, become a Christian. I wanted to say it to you three times.

Jew: I won't, I won't, I won't. And so I can also say it three times.

Rosso: I, Mister Jew, being the good fellow that I am, have done my duty and satisfied my conscience. But to tell you the truth I wouldn't give a snap of my fingers for anybody's soul. Now how much do you want for everything?

Jew: Twelve ducats.

Rosso: Of gold or in *carlini*?

Jew: According to the Roman practice, naturally.

Rosso: Turn around a little so that I can see how it looks in back.

Jew: There, I've turned around.

Rosso runs off with the cloak, and Romanello the Jew runs after him dressed as a friar.

Jew: Thief! Thief! Grab the thief! Block the thief!

A Bargello, or sheriff, arrives with some policemen:

49

Bargello: Stand still for the Law. What is this racket?

Rosso: Mr. Captain, this friar came out of the house of a whore, or from a tavern, drunk, and started to chase me, and I, not wishing to get mixed up with the clergy, started to flee. . . .

Jew: I am not a friar, I am Romanello a Jew and I want the cloak he has on his back.

Bargello: Oh you dirty, stinking dog, you make fun of our religion? Take him, tie him up, and put him in prison.

Rosso, despite his lack of religious convictions, has only contempt for the Jew Romanello—who doubtless returns the compliment. It is hard to imagine how Jews managed to live among Christians in those days, but there was a great amount of business done between the two communities, and the Eternal City was, as I have said before, considered to be a privileged place for Jews to live. The fictional character La Loçana andaluza, coming from a Spain that had expelled the Jews, is surprised to hear that Christians deal with them and that her Spanish sisters making a living in Rome consider them to be allies and friends. Jewish men could advance money for business enterprises, and Jewish women were known for their skill in preparing cosmetics and giving beauty treatments. Unlike their menfolk, the women were not required to wear a distinctive sign on their breasts.

Along with the city's more or less resident population was usually a very large number of transients—pilgrims (called *romei*), humanistic tourists, and simple seekers of adventure. The *Descriptio* lists a total of 236 hotels, inns, and taverns—a large figure for a city of 50,000. It is not possible to know how many visitors traveled to Rome during Pope Leo's pontificate. The papal diarist Paride dei Grassi says that 100,000 came in for the coronation alone, but that is surely exaggerated. It is probable, nevertheless, that visitors were usually very much in evidence, as they are in small tourist centers today. Pilgrims and tourists came to Rome either on horseback or on foot since Italian roads were not good enough for carriages. The city was eager to receive them. In the sixteenth century the principal hotels started sending boys to recruit guests at the Porta del Popolo, where most travelers entered the city. During that century also appeared the first fragmentary printed guides to Rome. They included particulars about indulgences granted for the visiting of certain shrines. There were doubtless also many human guides for hire.

Jacques Le Saige, a well-to-do merchant in the northern French city of Douai, undertook in 1518 a pilgrimage to Rome and the Holy Land. He traveled by horse, arriving in Rome after thirty-seven days, only a few of which had been spent in stopovers, on April 26. Along the way, he had noted the characteristics and prices of hotels in his diary. In Rome he stayed at an inn called The White Cross whose owner was from Douai. In just over a week of sightseeing, he took in the main marvels of the city—the Colosseum, the Vatican Palace, the Seven Churches, the Catacombs, the ruins of acqueducts, and the new palace of Agostino Chigi decorated by Raphael. He was impressed by nearly everything he saw and showed a remarkable credulity. Someone, perhaps an ignorant or cynical guide, convinced him that the acqueducts had once supplied Rome not only with water but also with olive oil and wine! At Saint Peter's, on different days, he witnessed two remarkable scenes.

51

On one day he had the good luck to see the ceremonies for the canonization of the French saint François de Paul: "It would not be possible to set down completely in writing the 'triumph' that was staged there. Because it was a wonder to be there and the ceremonies lasted quite four hours. And there were some people who paid half a *ducato* to see the said triumph."

On another day at the great basilica he saw a priest cast out four devils from a single woman. Each devil blew out a candle as he left the body of the victim! On the evening before his departure, Le Saige and three friends were admitted to the presence of the pope, who received them kindly and gave his blessing for their pilgrimage to the Holy Land. The good merchant left the Eternal City delighted with his visit and confirmed in the holy purpose of his journey.

Great numbers of Romans made their livings from caring for visitors. Others worked for the new residents and diplomats who had brought money with them. It is likely that, after government and ecclesiastical employment, what we call service occupations were the main source of income for the lower and middle classes. The major industry was building, also dependent principally on funds provided by the Church and wealthy newcomers. Twenty-five hundred men are supposed to have been at work on Saint Peter's at one time during the pontificate of Julius II. The construction of private palaces—of which the most important in this period was the Farnese—also required many workmen. A good proportion of the skilled ones had to be brought in from other cities.

The role of occupations modern economists consider really productive of wealth was small. Artisans—except those working in the building trade—were far fewer than in Florence, and even farming around Rome was less important than might be expected. The landowners had traditionally concentrated on raising animals for slaughter, and cultivation was neglected. During the sixteenth century grain for Rome had often to be imported from outside the Papal States. On the other side of the balance sheet, the city exported very little. Its economy was probably the least self-sufficient and least sound among those of large cities in Renaissance Europe. More even than the great capital cities of Northern Europe, it was dependent upon funds from the outside. A considerable part of the vast income of the Church was spent in Rome, either directly or through individuals. Indulgences were sold abroad to finance the building of Saint Peter's. Cardinals resident in Rome drew income from their titular ecclesiastical offices elsewhere. So, often, did writers and scholars, who had been granted benefices by the pontiff.

Like all dynamic and cosmopolitan cities where money is flowing and visitors are numerous, Rome attracted a large number of persons of questionable character who wished to earn a living with as little work as possible. Foreign beggars apparently came to the city in the hope that clergy and pilgrims would be easy marks. The government attempted to prevent them from encumbering the steps—and interiors—of churches. The beggars were popularly supposed, as at other times in history, to have formed guilds to regulate the exercise of their profession. Prostitutes were also present in Rome in extraordinarily high numbers, as we shall have occasion to see in the chapter on faith and morals. And there were doubtless many shady characters who simply waited in the streets for a dishonest opportunity. During the century, particularly after the beginning of the Counter-Reformation, the government made repeated efforts to control lawless elements in the city.

Two works of fiction already mentioned, Francisco Delicado's *La Loçana andaluza* and Aretino's *La Cortegiana*, give us apparently authentic glimpses into life among the lowest classes in Rome. The picture is far from complete, since honest working people are scarcely represented in these two exposé works, but the flavor of Rome as a cosmopolitan boom town is well rendered. La Loçana, heroine of Delicado's Spanish novel, comes to Rome in 1513 after mistreatment by her husband's family at home. She is an extremely adaptable and resourceful lady who is determined to make a new life for herself by whatever means come to hand. She soon meets a number of Spanish sisters who welcome her kindly and give her much useful information. She is initiated into Roman life also by Ranpín, or Rampino, an unprincipled young Italian whom she makes her partner. She eventually becomes a successful procuress and beautician, combining two naturally related trades.

Not long after arrival La Loçana meets another Spanish woman who is working as a laundress. The lady has lost most of her hair because, she thinks, of the humid atmosphere of the washhouse. (This explanation may, however, be erroneous, since it is implied that she suffers also from the French Disease.) When La Loçana speculates that there must be a lot of money in the laundry business, her new friend answers: "Ay! Señora! When I have to pay for the house and food and wood and ashes and soap and the pot and the jars and the baskets and water and clothes lines, and all the things needed in the house, what do you expect?"

This woman has her own business and employs two wash-women. She has to give them a lot of wine, because they seem to drink more than they work, and must cope with unfair competition by another Spanish woman who pretends to wash in the Spanish way but actually uses a cheaper Italian procedure. The differences between the two methods of laundry are explained as follows: "We soak [the clothes] and soap [them] and then put them in a basket and drain them, and the clothes stay there all night so the lye will run out, because otherwise the clothes would take on the color of the lye. And they [rival laundresses], when they soak the clothes, don't put in any soap and don't let the lye drain out, saying that it gets rid of the stains. And they put the ash back on the fire to cook a second time and then it has lost its strength."

We can appreciate the righteous indignation of this hard-working laundress who wishes to maintain the standards of honest craftsmanship. She is not, however, one of the "deserving poor," in the Victorian phrase, for she keeps two younger lovers on the string. These two men, one an Italian and the other a Spaniard, cause a strain on her cash budget because she must buy them gifts, but they, in turn, improve her style of life by bringing home food and other things they have stolen from their employers.

Aretino's play *La Cortegiana*, full of scoundrels and scabrous episodes, hardly represents a typical slice of Roman life. In the last act, however, the author has one of the characters deliver a serious attack on the treatment of servants in the great houses of Rome. It seems probable that Aretino himself worked as a servant during Pope Leo's time and that he knew well the conditions he was talking about. His spokesman in the play, the servant Rosso, is no saint, and the author too was often a dishonest and unreliable man. Yet the picture of servant life they give has the ring of truth. Rosso and the procuress Alvigia, accomplices in a swindle, have a little time on their hands while awaiting the results of their trickery, and he starts to tell her about the horrors of a servants' hall in a big house: "If bad luck forces you to go into a servants' hall, as soon as you enter you perceive a tomb so humid, so dark and so horrible that sepulchres are a hundred times more cheerful. And if you have seen the prison of Savella court when it is full of prisoners, you have seen the servants' hall full of servants at meal time because those who eat in the servants' hall resemble prisoners, as the hall resembles a prison. But prisons are considerably more pleasant than servants' halls because in winter prisons are as warm as in summer, while the halls boil in the summer and in the winter are so cold that your words freeze in your mouth. And the smell of the prison is less unpleasant than the stench of the hall because the first comes from men *living* in prison but the second from men *dying* in a servants' hall."

Rosso tells how miserly masters starve their servants, or give them food, such as rotten fruit or unseasoned bean soup, that can hardly be eaten. We are most shocked, however, by his descriptions of the filth that reigns in the servants' hall. The tablecloth is "of more colors than a painter's apron." Everyone drinks from one pewter cup "that all the water in the Tiber would not be able to wash clean." While eating the servants wipe their hands on their clothes or on the wall. In the summer there is a horrible smell from bone-piles covered with filth that are never swept away.

There is no doubt that servants in big houses often had a very hard life, and if all he says is true one hesitates to blame Rosso for having become such a rascal. The procuress Alvigia, to whom he tells these things, is, however, as shocked as modern readers, and, therefore, it would be hasty to assume that conditions were normally as bad as he paints them. The treatment of servants must have varied according to the humanity of the masters. And there is no reason to think they were any worse off in Rome than in other cities.

In the extreme demographic and social variety of Rome the cosmopolis, different ethnic groups and social classes had one thing in common: an almost unreasoning pride in the city's name. Native patrician and immigrant adventurer alike enjoyed thinking of all other cities as provincial, away from the center of things. We see now that much of the city's bustle—if one excepts the activity of artists—was sterile, and much of its prosperity insecure. Almost no one perceived these weaknesses at the time, however, and our perception of them today does not alter the fact that the air of High Renaissance Rome was that of a great city at a high point in its history.

POMP AND CIRCUMSTANCE

PUBLIC CEREMONIES and spectacles were of course more important in the sixteenth century than they are today. People had more time for them and were not yet affected by that cynical distrust of official solemnities characteristic of progressive Western nations today. Rome, in its double role as center of Christendom and capital of a secular state, may have offered more grand public entertainment than any other city of the Western world. An astonishing amount of artistic talent and effort was expended on such ephemeral manifestations, which were esteemed almost as much as lasting creations of painting, sculpture, and architecture. Romans were connoisseurs in these matters, and they expected proper entertainment from their rulers.

As in the time of the ancient emperors, public festivals were usually intended not only to afford artistic and theatrical pleasure but also to further the interests of the state. The interests of religion, of the Universal Church, were a new element since classical times, but they were seldom distinguished from those of state. This sometimes unfortunate confusion—not unknown in other societies of more recent times—was most evident in a triumphal entry into Rome of Julius II in March, 1507. The "Warrior Pope," as he is often called, was returning from a military campaign in which Bologna had been captured and returned to the States of the Church. He first spent a night at Santa Maria del Popolo, on the northern edge of the city, so that he could proceed solemnly to the Vatican next day. That day was, as it happened, Palm Sunday. After celebrating mass at Santa Maria, the pontiff started toward Saint Peter's. He passed many special decorations, among which arches of triumph were prominent. In front of each church along the way, Cardinals and other high clergy stood at temporary altars while choirs sang hymns. At the Castel Sant' Angelo there was a triumphal chariot drawn by four white horses. The chariot held a globe which served as base for a full-grown oak tree, and around the globe stood ten men waving palm branches. In this way they evoked both the triumphal return of victorious generals and Christ's entry into Jerusalem on Palm Sunday! When the pope finally arrived at the basilica of Saint Peter's after three hours, he prayed for a long time on the Apostle's tomb.

The first grand occasion of Leo's reign came on April 11, 1513, when he went to "take possession" of the Lateran Palace, still the official residence of the popes despite their recent preference of the Vatican. Accompanied by a numerous and colorful train of men-at-arms, ecclesiastical and civil officials, foreign ambassadors, and noble Romans and Florentines, the pope traversed the city on his white Arab stallion. The streets on the way had been specially decorated. The owners of private palaces had adorned the façades with rich draperies, with ancient statues in their collections, and with new works of art commissioned for the occasion. There were many arches of triumph, the most noted and remembered of these being one erected by the great Roman banker Agostino Chigi. It bore a Latin inscription that caught the public imagination:

"Olim habuit Cypris sua tempora; tempora Mavors
Olim habuit; sua nunc tempora Pallas habet."

("Once Venus had her time, then Mars; now Minerva will have hers.")

The new pope was expected to be a Minerva, a patron of the arts and sciences; the amorous Alexander had been a Venus, the belligerent Julius II a Mars. Once pontiffs were dead, the Roman populace no longer felt obliged to be respectful.

The most elaborate of public celebrations and artistic manifestations during Pope Leo's years came in September, 1513, when his brother and nephew were made honorary citizens of Rome. Detailed accounts of this *festa* have been left to us, and they are rich with direct or implied information about Roman civilization of the time. The festival was, from the intellectual point of view, a nearly perfect expression of the *Zeitgeist*, revealing both springs of creativity and follies. The pope had let it be known that he would like for his brother and nephew to be granted honorary citizenship, but the grand ceremonies and entertainments with which it was done were the idea of the city government rather than his own. It is no exaggeration to say that the city fathers were made ecstatic by the pope's request, which seemed to be a token of his high regard for Roman tradition and for the weak city government itself. Leo's early gestures of benevolence toward the Roman people had raised high hope for local prosperity and for a greater measure of autonomy. The delicacy of his new gesture is evidence of the superb command of diplomatic psychology with which historians credit him. No act of generosity toward the Romans could have delighted them in the same way as this apparently humble request for a favor. It implied that he took seriously their claim to be the genuine inheritors of the *Senatus Populus-Que Romanus*, that he did not share the condescension with which inhabitants of bustling cities like Florence and Venice were wont to view the old-fashioned Romans.

Giuliano was a very popular choice for the honor. He was from all accounts a cultivated and naturally kind gentleman beloved by his friends and hated by no one. He is one of the principal characters in Castiglione's *The Courtier*, set in Urbino just before Pope Leo's accession, and it may be said that he comes as near as anyone in that book to incarnating the social ideal of the author. Lorenzo, the other candidate for citizenship, was the son of the pope's dead brother Piero. He was disliked, as his father had been, and it was perhaps fortunate for the tone of the occasion that he was away in Florence and could not attend.

It was decided that the ceremonies would be held on the occasion of the *Palilia*, a pagan festival of the goddess Pales which was associated in late imperial times with the goddess Roma and the anniversary of the city's founding. Celebration of the *Palilia* had been revived, as we have seen, by the classicizing and paganizing members of Pomponius Laetus' Roman Academy. The solemnities and entertainments in Giuliano's honor could take place at only one place—at the city's civic center on the Capitoline Hill.

In classical times the hill had been crowned by a succession of temples to Jupiter, and in the city's religious life had played a role somewhat similar to that of the Acropolis in Athens. During the Middle Ages it had become a seat of government.

Though Michelangelo's fine Piazza del Campidoglio we know today did not exist in 1513, there were already two relatively unpretentious buildings bearing the names of Palazzo dei Conservatori and Palazzo del Senatore. No building seems to have existed on the site of the present Palazzo Nuovo, and one's view was clear to the medieval church of Aracoeli. There was an immense open space, not yet centering on the equestrian statue of Marcus Aurelius, which was kept at the Lateran. In this open space it was decided to construct an enormous classical theater of temporary materials just for the occasion. Some old walls had to be torn down, some ground had to be leveled, and the path leading up the hill had to be enlarged and put in good condition. The main façade of the theater was directed toward the path. It included six columns, with an arch between each pair. The middle arch contained the entrance to the theater; the other four were decorated with painted scenes from mythology or ancient history having to do with the Capitolium.

In the first arch on the right one could see the god Saturn, with a sickle on his shoulder, in the act of touching the hand of the two-faced god Janus. Both of these gods were supposed to have been residents of Rome in prehistoric times. Janus had lived on the Janiculum Hill, which is named for him. Saturn, arriving in Rome later, had been received cordially by Janus and had settled down on the Capitoline. The period of his residence in Rome had been that of the primitive golden age, the *saturnia regna* of Vergil and other poets. In this painting spectators saw an evocation of the legendary beginnings of Rome and also an intimation that Pope Leo and his brother would bring to the city a new golden age. In the second arch one could see the virgin Tarpeia being killed by the Sabines, to whom she had betrayed the Capitolium in expectation of a reward. In the fourth, past the door, one saw Romulus offering to Jupiter the spoils taken from Acrone, king of the Caenini in Latium. In the fifth was figured the Consul Horatius Pulvillus dedicating a temple to Jupiter on the Capitolium, remaining calm and going about his sacred business though his enemies had sent him a false message that his son was dead. This scene exalted the ancient (republican) virtue of stoicism.

Inside the building, at the far end, was another façade, with four columns. The spaces between columns were filled with paintings depicting, this time, significant moments or aspects of ancient relations between Romans and Etruscans. Latin inscriptions indicated the meaning of the scenes. Etruscan soldiers were shown welcoming Aeneas to Italy and helping him to found the empire. An Etruscan king was represented as reigning in Rome to the general satisfaction of the population. Roman youths were depicted as learning their letters from an Etruscan master. Etruscan actors were showing Romans the art of the stage. An Etruscan soothsayer demonstrated the craft of interpreting omens. By portraying in this way the real and imagined debts of Roman civilization to the Etruscan one, the artists did honor to Giuliano and his papal brother, since Florentines and other Tuscans sometimes considered themselves to be descendants of the Etruscans. They had little ground, really, for admiring Etruscan civilization, since much less was known about it then than is now, but they knew that it had antedated Rome, and that was enough reason for filial pride. It was particularly tactful of the Romans to acknowledge an ancient debt to Etruscan sooth-sayers and priests, since Tuscany had now sent a new priest to Rome. In the High Renaissance only rare people like Erasmus could be shocked at this promiscuity of pagan cults and Christianity!

One painting gave a more accurate indication of the his-torical relation of Florence to Rome. It showed the Trium-virate of Octavian, Anthony and Lepidus presiding over the building of the city of Florence. The scene was wholly imaginary, but Florence (unlike the neighboring village of Fiesole) had indeed started as a Roman colony, how-ever much sixteenth-century Florentines preferred to think of distinctive Etruscan origins.

One reporter of the festival, Paolo Palliolo, pauses after describing the theater in order to reflect lyrically upon the accomplishment of the architect, sculptors and painters who have made it: "I can't believe that Apelles, Zeuxis or Parrhasius or any . . . celebrated painter ever surpassed in elegance this noble work, which not only the people of Rome but a great multitude of foreigners rushed to see. It was examined by some old men who had not been out of their houses for a long time—and who may never come out of them again alive. Those who couldn't walk had them-selves carried. After having well inspected the whole, they confessed ingenuously never to have seen anything like it. Many Roman matrons and maidens, who are scarcely even allowed by their men to visit the temples [ancient ruins or churches?], were sent, along with small children, to see this theater."

The author compares the construction to a theater commissioned by the Consul Marcus Scaurus in 58 B.C., that is, in the most prosperous period of the Republic. The ancient one had also been temporary and built of wood but had had much greater dimensions. The author judges that the two accomplishments are comparable, but his reasoning reveals to us the wistful feelings of inferiority with which Romans of the Renaissance viewed their ancestors: "If one compares the immense abundance of infinite riches of those times with the present poverty, or indeed indigence, if one considers that that theater was built to receive for thirty days in a row the people of Rome then so numerous and this one [to receive] the two Magnificences [Giuliano and Lorenzo] for two days, and especially if we think that while . . . Marcus Scaurus' father was a prince of Rome when she was ruler of peoples and received, along with Marius, the booty of the provinces, and that he [the son] built his theater of enormous size and stupendous with ornaments of spoils gathered from all over the world, so that no one since has been able to equal it, and if one considers that this present Roman posterity, disheartened and reduced to such an extent that (if we are ashamed to confess what is a fact) it is not even master of itself, made the theater of the quality we have shown from the proceeds of the tax immunities granted to it by Leo X, then I say we will judge that this [theater] is no less memorable and marvelous for its time than that of Marcus Scaurus was for his."

Renaissance Italians—and particularly Romans—had the

66

impression that they were less accomplished than their classical ancestors not only in artistic and philosophical affairs but also in practical ones and in their general standard of living. It is as though present-day Americans looked back to the Jeffersonian Age as a time superior in art, letters, virtue, and *technology.*

The chronicler Palliolo states that a host of artists and architects came to admire the building and, unable to tear themselves away, made drawings of all its parts and took many measurements. There is no way of knowing how many had actually contributed to the work. We know from the art historian Vasari that Baldassare Peruzzi was the painter of the tableau showing Tarpeia, and he may well have done or supervised some of the others. His is the only well-known name that can be assigned with sureness to the project. The architect was a relatively unknown man, the Tuscan Pietro Rosselli. Artistic talent and inspiration were, however, so plentiful in the Rome of Leo X that one should not infer from the absence of famous names that the project was not a masterpiece.

The stage and some rows of seats were covered with fine rugs. Giuliano and his company arrived at the Campidoglio on the morning of September 13. The theater was already filled with spectators. His Magnificence was greeted by officials of the Roman civic government and by ambassadors of France, Spain, the Holy Roman Empire, Milan, Florence, and other states. One of the dignitaries, the Despot of Morea, became so angry at not being given ceremonial precedence over the ambassador of Emperor Maximilian I that he retired in a huff to the Palazzo dei Conservatori (and remained to watch the festivities from there). It is hard to imagine why this exiled ruler of a

67

minor country in the hands of the Turks should have considered himself due precedence over the Imperial ambassador. Perhaps, as a sovereign, even in exile, he felt superior to all ambassadors, or perhaps as a member of the Paleologus family he claimed to represent the whole occupied Eastern Empire centered at Constantinople and considered the Holy Roman emperors of the west as upstarts. Some of the Greek exiles in Italy had astonishing pretensions. One of them, the king of Cyprus, was hilariously satirized in 1521, when jokers designed a medal supposedly bearing his device. It showed a castle in the air, with a motto taken from the New Testament: "My kingdom is not of this world."

The assembly first heard a mass celebrated by the Bishop of Aquila. Then there was a Latin oration touching upon the distinction of the Medici family, the past greatness of Rome, and hopes for its future. Giuliano was commended for having understood the value of Roman citizenship. He responded in a few words and was then presented with a certificate of blue parchment with gold letters. It was now three hours since he had arrived at the Campidoglio. He and other dignitaries retired into the Palazzo dei Conservatori to rest while the stage was being prepared for the banquet.

This banquet is one of the few from the Renaissance for which we have a complete listing of courses. There were more than twenty of them, each announced by the sounding of trumpets, and the company remained at table for at least four hours—six according to one source. Important Roman citizens had lent gold and silver dishes, displayed on a large credenza, and glassware and napkins were of the finest quality. The guests sat down and washed their hands in scented water. They found napkins folded to form tents, and when these were undone small birds flew out. The birds were tame, and many stayed on the tables during the meal, amusing the guests by their antics.

The first course consisted of sweetmeats—a strange beginning to modern European and American taste, but not an uncommon one at various times in history. Most of the other courses featured roast meats. There was one very peculiar invention of serving which may have been inspired by classical Roman accounts. A large number of animals were served *rivestiti*, that is, "redressed." They had been skinned carefully and cooked whole; then their skins —uncooked, one presumes—had been put back on them and sewn together. The animals were arranged in natural postures and brought in on large trays. They thus looked for all the world as though they were not only uncooked but alive. Animals served in this way included peacocks, a calf, a boar, a deer, and an eagle carrying a rabbit in his talons. Among other interesting dishes one notes roast kids stuffed with roast birds, testicles of roosters, gilded calves' heads with lemons in their mouths, and big pastry balls (*palle* from the Medici coat of arms) that contained live rabbits. There was a great deal of fruit, as was natural in September, but very little in the way of vegetables.

Throughout the meal, "odors" burned under the tables. At one point servants brought in a large artificial mountain that had on each side a spring flowing with scented water. The guests rose and washed their hands under the springs. Ice and snow, brought from the mountains at great inconvenience, were also carried round. Buffoons moved about constantly, cutting capers and making jokes. At length, when the guests had eaten all they could manage, they became restless: "Things started to be thrown around, and one saw goats, rabbits, suckling pigs, capons, pheasant, and partridges flying through the air, so that the whole interior of the theater was full of them."

The banquet ended at last, and the distinguished guests retired to the palace to rest while the stage was being cleared. Then they returned to watch a pageant. Its various skits had been written, and were produced, by local Roman *letterati*, probably all connected with the Roman Academy or the *studio*, and the roles—male and female—were played by young men of good family. The first skit presented a beautiful lady crowned with gold who was the Dea Roma. Roma, accompanied by her nymphs, is delighted to see her city's fortunes improving again, and she is very happy to have received such an illustrious new son. These characters having retired, there entered on the stage two *villani*, or peasants, actors in a small drama that combined the gracious classical traditions of the eclogue with pointed contemporary allusions. These peasants also recite in Latin! One of them had come to live near Rome because in another province soldiers had burned his house and abducted his wife and sister. Now, in Latium, he has had his grape crop stolen by thieves just before harvest time. He is bent upon violent revenge: "But since it avails me nothing to excommunicate them or to complain to [abstract] reason, and they are not afraid of the pillory, I mean to chase them with arrows and, if I can catch them, I have decided to cut off their nose and ears and go to live among the Turks, since I can't get any rest in the Latin country."

The other peasant has had his donkey, his mare, and his wood stolen. They hit upon the idea of going to put their cases before the *conservatori* of the city government, since these gentlemen aren't dishonest like the other courts of Rome, "where lawyers with a flying quill write three words *et cetera . . .* and ask for money." Arriving at the Campidoglio, the two farmers had stumbled on the celebrations and had been so carried away by the public exaltation that they had hurried home to find gifts for Giuliano. They have returned bringing rustic gifts—chickens, eggs, and perch—and a friend who plays the guitar.

The third skit presented the *dio capitolino,* or god of the capitol. When first arriving on the stage he appears as an old man, but after seeing the joyous revival of civic life on his hill, he sheds his white hair and beard and takes on a youthful appearance. He remarks that the celebrations must be in honor of a god since no mortal would be worthy of them. Giuliano and his brother the pope must be from the stock of Medici whose coming had been predicted by Jupiter. The god hazards the prediction that under the new pontiff the "toga-clad people" will regain their *imperium.*

Meanwhile, inside the theater, crowding had become severe. So many gentlemen had moved up to sit on the stage that there was scarcely room for the actors. Outside, a large portion of the Roman population was trying to gain entrance. The door was guarded by soldiers with pole-axes, and we are told that: "They did not allow to enter just any artisan or vile plebian but only those whom they judged from their looks to be worthy of such entertainment." But some artisans and vile plebians scaled the walls and watched the goings on from above.

The final skit of the evening featured ladies (or disguised young men) representing Rome and Florence in the company of Cybele, mother of the gods. Florentia quarrels bitterly with Roma, accusing her of stealing a distinguished Florentine citizen. Recalling the past greatness of Rome, when all men of talent had gravitated to her, Florence terms her "insatiable" and "the depopulator of the world." The younger city is asked truculently in turn whether she recalls having been the "pupil" of Rome. At last Florentia is reconciled to having Giuliano become a *civis romanus*. During this number medals commemorating his citizenship had been passed out to the crowd. Music had been provided by corybantes, who were members of the orchestra of Ippolito Cardinal d'Este.

The pageant was not yet completed, but those in charge decided to put off the remainder until the morrow because of the late hour. Giuliano was seen home with one hundred torches. He returned the next afternoon and the pageant was resumed. In the final act appeared Clarice Orsini dei Medici, deceased wife of Lorenzo the Magnificent and mother of the pope and Giuliano. It was inevitable that this lady should be evoked during the celebrations, for she had constituted the first link between the Medici and the city of Rome. As a member of the illustrious Roman house of the Orsini, she had been from the point of view of social ambition an excellent match for Lorenzo, whose family, though wealthy, was of recent distinction. Clarice is represented in the pageant as having come down from Heaven —from the region of the Big Bear (Ursa = Orsini), to be precise. She is accompanied by the Arno and the Tiber, river gods, and is herself called a goddess at one point. She declares that she had carried a lion (Leo) in her womb and that in giving birth to him she had been like another Leto, mother of Apollo, since she too had been giving a sun to the world. The Tiber ventures a very rash set of predictions for the success of Pope Leo's reign. The new pontiff will give eternal peace to Italians and his feet will be kissed by people not only of the Mediterranean but also "of the farthest Ocean." He will free the eastern and southern Mediterranean shores of Turkish rule: "He will return to Troy with war in favor of the Greeks who are calling on him and he will purge happy Asia with our river and will also cleanse Babylon of its wickedness, and vain superstition will be cast upon the ground and the African people will be baptized." These predictions seem naïve in our hind-sighted awareness of Church crisis and of the increased prosperity of the Ottoman Empire, but optimism was in the Roman air in 1513.

When the pageant was finished, preparations were made for the playing of Plautus' comedy *Poenulus*—in Latin. This was one area of creative achievement in which Romans could justly claim primacy. The classicists of the Roman Academy and *studio* had presented not only Plautus and Terence but also the tragedian Seneca. Tommaso Inghirami, who filled the former chair of the great Pomponius Laetus, bore the nickname of "Fedra" in memory of a distinguished youthful performance as that lady in Seneca's *Hippolytus*. It was he who directed our performance of *Poenulus*. All the roles—men and women, youths and old people—were played by young men. A chronicler tells that they were all dressed in the height of young men's fashions, without regard for the age or sex of the characters they were playing. Their pronunciation and deliveries were magnificent. It was obvious that they had been "born and nourished in the fountain of Latium." Florentines could not have done half so well!

Poenulus ("The Carthaginian") is a typical example of classical comedy, learned by the Romans from the Greek

Menander and passed on by them to the Italians of the Renaissance. (Classical comedy written in Italian was still in its infancy in 1513, though its two best authors, Machiavelli and Ariosto, were already writing in Florence and Ferrara.) The plot of *Poenulus* is, characteristically, a story of young love, frustrated at first but finally triumphant. The comic elements include both farcical situations and ridiculous stock characters. The denouement is brought about by frankly unlikely occurrences.

One cannot resist speculating on how many of the Latin lines were understood by the dignitaries present. Some people, especially the Romans who had been Fedra's students, may have understood almost everything. Most, including the good Giuliano, must have missed over half of what they heard. Did they pretend to understand when they did not, laughing self-consciously when it seemed appropriate, like Americans with two years of college French who attend a Molière play? In a sense, however, a detailed understanding of the lines was no more necessary here than at the opera today. Costume and gesture were entertainment enough.

Pope Leo heard such lavish praises of the pageant and the play that he had both put on again at the Vatican a few days later. The Romans were inordinately proud of what they had done. Several Latin poems commemorated the occasion. Pope Leo was moved to new benevolence toward the *SPQR*: he reduced the tax on salt and conceded more powers to the city government. He also gave his blessing to having the *Palilia* celebrated annually.

There were of course many regular religious festivities and observances in Rome. On certain days relics or images of the Virgin and saints were carried through the streets amid great demonstrations of piety by the populace. This was done also on some exceptional occasions. Thus in 1517, after hearing of a Turkish victory, Leo X, accompanied by the highest clergy bearing relics, walked barefoot from Saint Peter's to Santa Maria sopra Minerva to beg God for deliverance from the peril of Islam.

The annual festivities with the greatest popular appeal were naturally those of Carnival, just preceding Lent. They included entertainment on various levels, announced in advance and approved by the government. People were allowed on certain designated days to go about in masks, provided they bore no arms and refrained from certain practical jokes such as throwing egg shells filled with water. There was a whole series of street races. On one day boys and young men ran, on another old men (with a top age of sixty), and on another the Jews. The last doubtless ran unwillingly, and their race may have been a cruel spectacle. Carnival also featured one or more so-called "hunts" of bulls and wild animals, in which young men of good family demonstrated their courage. On a higher plane, in Piazza Navona, then called Agone, there was a parade of elaborately costumed notables and of decorated chariots or floats. In 1515 the floats were decorated under the direction of Tommaso Inghirami, whom we have just seen as producer of the comedy on the Campidoglio. The chariots represented abstract virtues such as Friendship, Mildness, and Magnanimity. (At other times, it seems, there were satirical floats with allusions to living persons.) The ephemeral artistic creations of Carnival have undoubted descendants in our college-homecoming decorations and county fair parades. In the Italian Renaissance, however, the most gifted of artists gave their talents, and the result

75

must have been far superior to things of the sort we see today.

The arrival of foreign embassies provided stirring entertainment for the court and for many inhabitants of the city. There were stately processions through the streets of brilliantly costumed dignitaries and men-at-arms. The processions passed over the Bridge of Sant' Angelo on their way to the Vatican, and the pope often watched them from the battlements of that fortress. He would then return to the palace through a raised passageway in time to receive the embassy. The grandest such procession was provided by the ambassadors of King Manuel I of Portugal in March, 1514. That little country was then in the most glorious period of its history, sponsoring voyages of exploration and acquiring footholds for trade at numerous places in Africa and the Orient. King Manuel made much of the fact that he was carrying Christianity to heathen lands, and this argument made a very favorable impression upon the pope.

The chief of the embassy arriving in Rome on March 12, 1514, was Tristan da Cunha, himself an accomplished sailor and explorer. He and his companions had brought many gifts, the most interesting of these being exotic animals—a female leopard, a fine jennet horse, parrots and other unusual fowl, and a white elephant. The last animal, none of whose species had been seen in Rome since classical times, was the star of the parade. He was led by one Moorish keeper and another sat on his neck. He carried a jeweled howdah on his back. On his hindquarters sat the leopard. One can imagine the excitement of the people in the streets. At one point along the way the elephant was given water. He drank part of it and sprayed the rest playfully on nearby spectators. At last he arrived at the bridge in front of Castel Sant' Angelo, from which Pope Leo was watching with his spyglass. The elephant then knelt, bowed his head reverently, and saluted the head of the Church with blasts of his trumpet: "Bar! Bar! Bar!" This beast, who bore the Carthaginian name of Hanno, was immediately famous. Much poetry was written about him, and Raphael painted his portrait (now destroyed). His death in 1516 caused much grief to the papal household and the citizens of Rome.

The Roman people were in sum well entertained and often edified and educated in the process. The richness of public ceremonies and artistic manifestations bound the Romans together in a civic pride as strong as that found in republican city-states. The population was moreover still small enough for a majority—at least of men—to be present at all grand public occasions. And as a result there was little psychological alienation between rulers and ruled, whatever the injustices of the political and social systems.

THE LIFE OF LETTERS

THE CARDINAL dei Medici had been a patron of letters before his elevation to the papacy, keeping a sort of literary salon in his town house (the present Palazzo Madama, largely changed in exterior appearance). When he was elected, jubilant poets and scholars hailed the dawn of a new golden age of literature. The glorious predictions contained an element of moral blackmail, since the new pope would feel obliged to do his part—especially his financial part—in making them come true. Many writers rushed to Rome and to the Vatican in order to seek his patronage. He was to be importuned by begging literary men for the rest of his life and must sometimes have wished that his reputation as a Maecenas were less widespread.

His efforts to promote the writing of good literature were, in the event, sincere, but often unsystematic and undiscriminating. Modern critics have taken pleasure in pointing out that the celebrated Age of Leo X was not, in Rome, productive of literary masterpieces. Ariosto and Machiavelli, the best writers of the time, both had some connection with the pope and the Medici family, but their works belong to Ferrara and Florence. Baldassare Castiglione was an occasional member of literary circles in Rome, and his *The Courtier* was partly written there, but it is forever associated with the little court of Urbino. And yet, despite the dearth of great works, the High Renaissance in Rome was undoubtedly a brilliant period in the history of literature. It was brilliant because of the size and distinction of its literary society, by the quality of what the French call *la vie littéraire*.

This literary life was not only very different from any we know today but also different, in many ways, from any existing elsewhere in Europe at the same time. Much of its peculiar quality derived from a unique and extremely complex linguistic situation. High Renaissance Rome did not have a single, standard language. Most of the residents spoke some form of Italian—though there were many Spaniards, Frenchmen, and Germans—but the native dialect of the city was very different from the Florentine of Pope Leo and his countless friends from home. As for writing, it was done in Latin, in Florentine, in Roman dialect, and in various versions of a supposed Italian koine called *lingua cortigiana* or *lingua italica*. As always when citizens of one state speak and write more than one tongue, feelings ran high on linguistic questions. There were lively quarrels among literary men, and even among men on the streets. Several documents concerning these quarrels have been preserved—testifying to their importance—and we can reconstruct the most common arguments used by the various factions.

The most fundamental, though not the liveliest, quarrel was between Latinists and partisans of the literary vernacular. In the Rome of the early sixteenth century, Latin made a last stand as the language of general culture. It was a brave last stand, characterized by assurance and even by arrogance. Latin was not only the official language of the Church and of the *comune* but also the most common medium of scholarship and, for the city of Rome, the principal language of belles-lettres. The native aristocracy were almost as much interested in promoting the use of Latin as the Church was. Their dialect of Italian had been the vehicle for no masterpieces in literature, and they were no match for Florentines in vernacular culture. How natural, then, to hark back to classical times, when Rome had been the *caput mundi*, and to pretend that vernacular accomplishments were inferior. Latin was not the spoken language of the city, but it was not entirely confined to the written page. It was often heard—in sermons and other orations, in classical plays, in recited poetry, in university instruction, and even, at times, in conversation. The pope was wont, for example, to reply extemporaneously in Latin to the prepared greetings of ambassadors.

What arguments did the champions of Latin have on their side? From the vantage point of today we see easily that the soundest one was far and away that of universality. Latin could be read by educated men all over Europe, as no form of Italian could. The Latinists did not emphasize this advantage enough, nor did they point it out in a sufficiently direct manner. Ercole Strozza, the gentleman who is made to defend Latin in Bembo's *Prose della volgar lingua* (1525), argues as follows: "For the Latin language is but one language, of a single quality and form, with which all the Italian peoples and others who are not Italian write in a single way . . . so that I, setting out to write Latin, could not err in choosing in my standard.

But the vernacular is different. Because, although all the peoples who are included within the boundaries of Italy talk and speak vernacularly, nevertheless Neapolitan men speak vernacularly in one way, and in another the Lombards talk, and in another the Tuscans. . . . if I wished to write vernacularly, I wouldn't know how to choose a model among so many forms . . . of vernacular tongues." Strozza's friends are able to show, however, that a standard kind of Italian can be developed. The fact that international communication will still be a problem is passed over.

Nor do Latinists seem to have made much capital of the fact that writing in the ancient language placed one in a tradition nearly two thousand years old. They were inclined to put the main emphasis on a difference of quality between Latin and the vernaculars. Modern students of the Romance languages would be astonished to hear that some Latinists scorned these tongues on the ground that they had no grammar. By this strange statement were meant two quite different things: first, that spelling and syntax were not codified and, second, that there were fewer conjugated verb forms than in the classical languages and no noun declensions at all. Virtually no one, in the infancy of historical philology, understood the process of evolution from a synthetic language to analytic ones, a process by which flexional endings tended to be replaced by new constructions with prepositions and auxiliary verbs.

There was indeed serious dispute over the central fact of the Romance languages' descent from Latin. The people who said that Italian was a decayed form of Latin were nearest the truth, wrong only in the pejorative implication of the adjective "decayed." (One called Spanish a Latin that had lost its teeth, and another termed Italian a Latin that had fallen into its second childhood.) Gian Giorgio Trissino, prominent writer in Rome under Leo X, thought that Italian had derived much of its phonology from Greek during the period of Byzantine dominance. Italian was thus "Latin by birth and Greek by education." One may marvel most of all at the contention of some proud Florentines, anxious not to be indebted to Rome, who claimed that the tongue of Dante derived not from Latin but from ancient Etruscan. And there were other bizarre theories that confused the whole question.

What, on the other hand, were the principal arguments of the defenders of Italian as a language of literature and (more rarely) of scholarship? The only valid one—and the only one needed, it turned out—was the observation that Italian was the maternal language of local writers and that Latin had to be acquired artificially. Little was made of the corollary to this observation, that is, that far more people in Italy could understand the vernacular than could understand Latin. The age was aristocratic, and there was little impulse to educate the masses. Real concern was shown for only one class of people who did not know Latin —well-born ladies. Much lyric poetry had already been written in Italian for their benefit, and treatises dealing with love, for example, Bembo's *Asolani*, were in the vernacular as well. And if, in the Age of Leo X, Roman poets persisted in addressing their loves in the language of Horace and Catullus, one must assume that they wished to be read only by their colleagues.

To the charge that Italian was incapable of expressing great thoughts, Florentines replied by pointing to the success of Dante, Petrarch, and Boccaccio in the great *trecento*. Romans must have grown as weary of hearing about these three men as Florentines were of being told of the uninterrupted classical tradition of Rome.

High Renaissance Latinists were themselves divided into two opposing factions—Ciceronians and eclectics. This quarrel, though of great intellectual importance in the whole of Europe, need not be considered directly here because the Romans were all fanatical Ciceronians. The leader of the other camp, the great Erasmus, was far away in Northern Europe. (His caustic observations about Ciceronianism in Rome will, however, concern us in another connection.)

The partisans of the vernacular had time on their side, though their general triumph in Italy was still well into the future. Among themselves they carried on another linguistic quarrel which was a good deal livelier, if less fundamental, than the one with the Latinists. It set the haughty Florentines and other Tuscans, on one side, against jealous men from the rest of Italy on the other. Florentine was well on its way to becoming the basis of the literary language, but this fact was disputed, and there was also fierce resistance. Italy was not a nation like France or England. Differences between Italian dialects were— and are—enormous. Even today illiterate people from the north and the south cannot carry on a conversation with each other. The Roman dialect was much closer to southern Italian dialects in the early sixteenth century than it is now; today's *romanesco* has been greatly influenced by Florentine—less, perhaps, through education than through Tuscan immigration to Rome. Much of that immigration took place during the pontificates of the two Medici. The Florentines who came to the Eternal City in the train of Leo X were intolerant of the language spoken by the na-

tives, and their arrogance must often have been insuffer-
able.

Piero Valeriano, in a dialogue about the language question, has an elderly Roman gentleman express the resentment of his countrymen: "My situation is pitiful; every
time I need to write a few words to a friend [I have to
decide] whether I am to use my own language or send out
to the butcher for another one. . . . I can no longer walk
around in the Parione quarter. Those young doctors with
the little beards . . . come out and listen to what we are
talking about and note down accents, words, or figures that
are not Tuscan, and then they abuse us without any com-
passion at all because we don't know something that we
never dreamed of needing to learn. I don't deny that, since
we have a Tuscan prince, endowed with such virtue, learning, and kindness, one should strive . . . to do something
that would please him. But I, a poor old man, how can I
so quickly forget a language that I've used for fifty to
sixty years and learn a new one, especially since, as you
see, my teeth are starting to fall out. I just don't know what
to do . . . since I don't speak Tuscan, and say *mi* and *ti*,
except leave Rome." The old gentleman is assured by his
friends that the pontiff is personally quite tolerant in linguistic matters, though he enjoys all the controversy.

A chauvinistic Florentine also takes part in Valeriano's
dialogue, and, though his arguments are rejected, he is
permitted a few clever remarks. He says, for example, that
Florentine is secure in its own beauty but that other Italian
dialects are taking words and constructions from Latin because they need borrowed adornment if they are to appear
as "ladies" rather than as "peasant women." An opponent
replies in the same vein that by moving away from Latin,

85

Florentines have made their language into a "disgusting whore" rather than a "venerable lady."

Piero Valeriano, the author of the dialogue, was an anti-Florentine who favored taking as literary language the *lingua cortigiana*, a sort of cultured koine supposedly spoken at Italian courts, especially at that of Rome. (This language, in so far as it existed, was probably based in reality upon Florentine.) A similar view was held by Trissino, who wished the common language to be called Italian or "Italic" (and who proposed some controversial reforms in spelling), and also by Baldassare Castiglione, author of *The Courtier*. Pietro Bembo, in his *Prose della volgar lingua*, favored taking the archaic Florentine of the *trecento* as a basis for the national language; by rejecting much of the current spoken Florentine, however, he showed that as a Venetian he too resented the arrogance of the pope's countrymen. In Florence itself, Machiavelli stood up for the living language of his city.

This quarrel was doubtless carried on also in non-literary milieux, for there are few possessions more sacred to a man than his language. Aretino, in his satirical and obscene *Ragionamenti*, has one Roman courtesan tell about another, nicknamed *Madrema non vuole* ("Mama doesn't want me to"), who is a Florentine purist in linguistic matters and corrects people who speak badly: "She makes fun of everyone who doesn't speak according to the standard; and she says that one must say *balcone* and not *finestra*, *porta* and not *uscio*, *tosto* and not *vaccio*, *viso* and not *faccia*, *cuore* and not *core*, *miete* and not *mete*, *percuote* and not *picchia*, *ciancia* and not *burla*." "Mama doesn't want me to" apparently concerned herself both with vocabulary and with pronunciation.

The intense literary activity of Leonine Rome may be divided into three imperfectly distinct spheres: the official, the private and aristocratic, and the popular. The official literature was very largely Latin, since the use of that language was favored both by the Vatican and the Campidoglio. As soon as Pope Leo was elected, he announced the appointment of two Latin secretaries, Pietro Bembo and Jacopo Sadoleto. Both were distinguished Ciceronian Latinists, and their job was to cast the pope's official letters in the most elegant Latin possible. An ancient Roman would find the form of their letters rather familiar, though he would be puzzled by some direct references to Christ and by the deference shown to upstart potentates and political entities such as the *Rex gallorum* and the *Illustrissimum dominium venetum.* The pope was also the deliberate or casual patron of much Latin oratory. Public address was a far more esteemed branch of literature than it is today, and particularly so in Rome, where the educated native population fancied that they had inherited the correct Latin pronunciation. Erasmus, who visited the city during the pontificate of Julius II, tells in the satirical *Ciceronianus* of having been urged to attend a Latin sermon on the death of Christ so that he might have the unrivaled treat of hearing "how Roman speech sounds in a Roman mouth."

His account of the sermon touches on more fundamental matters than linguistic ones: "I went eagerly, I stood next to the platform, not to lose anything. Julius II was present in person. . . . A crowded assembly of cardinals and bishops was there and many scholars who were then living in Rome, besides the common throng. I shall not mention the name of the speaker. . . . He . . . was a candidate for Ciceronianism. The introduction and peroration, longer almost than the real sermon, were occupied in proclaiming the praises of Julius II, whom he called Jupiter Optimus Maximus holding and brandishing in his powerful right hand the three-cleft and fatal thunderbolt and causing by a mere nod whatever he wished. All that had been done in France, Germany, Spain, Portugal, Africa, and Greece, he declared, had been done by the will of Julius alone. So spoke at Rome a Roman in Roman tongue and Roman style."

"But what had this characterization to do with Julius, the high priest of the Christian religion, vice-regent of Christ, successor of Peter and Paul? What with cardinals and bishops performing the duty of other apostles? . . . In so Roman a fashion spoke that Roman that I heard nothing about the death of Christ. And yet, he was a most ambitious candidate for Ciceronian eloquence and seemed to Ciceronians to have spoken wonderfully, though he said almost nothing on the subject, which he seemed neither to know nor to care for, nothing to the point, and moved no one's feelings. He merited only this praise that he had spoken like a Roman and had reproduced something of Cicero."

Ciceronian eloquence in church was probably at least as much in favor under Pope Leo X. In the diary of the pope's master of ceremonies, Paride de' Grassi, one finds the following entry for the year 1517: "On the day of Saint John, in the papal chapel, in the presence of the Pope with all the cardinals . . . [a cardinal] . . . celebrated the mass and the sermon was given by a certain scholar from Narni, more in the gentile fashion than in the Christian. He invoked [the immortal] gods and goddesses in an exclamation, so that many people laughed and many became angry.

The Pope patiently tolerated [the blunder] in keeping with his very patient and very kind nature."

Referring to the deity in the plural was both the most natural and the most dangerous error that Christian Ciceronians could make. The set formulae of classical Latin solemnity and poetry were not appropriate for an age of monotheism, but a writer's aesthetic sense might be offended at the idea of invoking "God" instead of the classical "immortal gods." Some ancient deities could—and did —survive as purely literary conventions, but might ministers of the Church, or any official writers and orators, indulge in such conventions? The question was a thorny one.

The domain of official literature included an astonishing production of occasional poetry, most of it also in Latin. Verses were whipped out to celebrate Julius's victories, Leo's accession, the gift of the elephant from the king of Portugal, the reception of King Henry VIII's tasteful Latin work, *Defense of the Seven Sacraments against Martin Luther,* and many other events. Though the authors had no commissions, they were often writing for money because they hoped to be rewarded. They tried to get a copy of their work brought to the pope's attention and, if possible, to get a chance to read it aloud to him. Accounts of the court indicate that, though Pope Leo's nearsightedness prevented him from doing a great amount of reading, he had an almost unlimited patience for listening to Latin hexameters. Such patience was not uncommon. A modern scholar of the period, Domenico Gnoli, has suggested that many humanists derived a sensual pleasure from Latin declamation that had little to do with the sense of the words. That would explain the high praise given to some works that seem to us of low merit. When Pope Leo was pleased—most of the time, it would seem—he had an attendant dip into a bag of money and hand some to the poet. If his pleasure was more profound, he might have the man added to the papal payroll.

The pontiff was also interested in hearing light, improvised verse, particularly at dinner, and we may, somewhat paradoxically, include this sort of production among official literature. The best remembered of the many improvisers is Camillo Querno, an "archpoet" whom the pope liked to have near him in the evening. He was a great drinker and joker, a sort of Roman Falstaff. The pontiff is said sometimes to have required him to improvise six verses before the serving of each course. If he did badly, water was put into his wine. On one famous occasion, Pope Leo improvised a hexameter in reply to him. Querno had boasted:

> *Archipoeta facit versus pro mille poetis.*
> (The archpoet makes verses for a thousand poets.)

The pope rejoined:

> *Et pro mille aliis archipoeta bibit.*
> (And the archpoet drinks for a thousand others.)

This quick reply was cited as proof of extraordinary wit and culture.

An earlier archpoet had been victim of a cruel hoax that delighted the literary society of all Italy. Baraballo, an abbot from Gaeta, was a facile poet and man of naïve vanity, and jokers at court praised his work in order to enjoy his fatuous credulity. It was decided to have him crowned with laurel on the Campidoglio—after the example of Petrarch! He was to ride there from the Vatican on the back of the elephant Hanno. Poor Baraballo did not realize that he was being made ridiculous. His family did understand and tried, in vain, to prevent the affair. Everyone, apparently, was in on the joke except the victim. He appeared before Pope Leo, dressed in green velvet and ermine, to read some verses. Other poets present read their own verses in praise of him. At length he descended to the courtyard and mounted the elephant, who had been decorated for the occasion. He proceeded to the Sant' Angelo Bridge, observed and cheered by a large part of the Roman population, but there Hanno threw off his rider. One may admire today, in the Vatican's Sala della Segnatura, a representation in inlaid wood of Baraballo on the elephant.

Another victim of the scholarly malice of Roman *letterati* was an ambitious teacher named Giulio Simone Siculo. He had contrived to publish an account of the Capitoline celebrations of 1513 four days after they had taken place. This journalistic accomplishment would not be remarkable if the author had written in prose, but he had composed four hundred Latin hexameters. Pope Leo was apparently pleased with Siculo's spirit of enterprise and awarded him a well-paid professorship. Other professors and literary men were horrified, since Siculo's poetry was understandably lacking in quality and originality. They got together —seventy-two of them—and composed a satirical scholarly commentary on the "masterpiece," with many learned and malicious observations. An accompanying biography of the famous poet provides the information that he descends distantly from a union of Polyphemus and a nanny goat, and immediately from that of a priest and a nun. Pietro

Bembo and Jacopo Sadoleto, Latin secretaries of the pope, participated in this light-hearted project.

The highest aspiration that one could have in Neo-Latin literature—and also in the vernacular—was to create a modern epic comparable to the epics of Homer and Vergil. Petrarch, the first modern with such ambitions, had expended immense time and energy on his Latin epic *Africa*, about the Roman hero Scipio Africanus, and he expected to be immortal for that work rather than for his Italian lyric poetry. Other humanistic writers followed his example in similar projects. Pope Leo knew that only a classical epic —preferably on a Christian theme—could crown his pontificate in literature and raise his reputation as a patron to the level of that of Augustus. Marco Girolamo Vida, made prior of a monastery in the nearby village of Frascati, worked on such a poem with the pope's warm encouragement.

The finished work, called the *Christias*, or *Christiad*, was published only in 1535, fourteen years after the pontiff's death, but it may be considered a product of the Leonine Age. In six books of Latin hexameters the poet recounts Christ's career from the journey to Jerusalem with the disciples through the performing of miracles, the Crucifixion, a descent into Limbo, the Resurrection, and the granting of the Holy Spirit to the disciples. Flashbacks evoke the birth of Christ and His childhood, and at the end one has a glimpse at the future victories of Christianity. As the *Aeneid* had contained back-dated predictions of the greatness of the Roman Empire, so this Christian epic predicts the greatness of Rome as seat of the Church. The poem includes many classical allusions, and the poet has Christ, after His crucifixion, make the acquaintance in Limbo of several famous and just pagans. But, unlike many of his contemporaries, Vida is careful not to glorify pagan religion by equating it with Christianity. God the Father is referred to classically as *Summus Parens* or *Supernus Pater* but he is not called *Jupiter Optimus Maximus*. The epic, almost totally forgotten today, like most Neo-Latin literature, is supposed to have influenced both Tasso and Milton.

The official literature centering around the Roman university, or *studio*, and the Campidoglio was mostly oratorical. We may obtain an idea of its flavor, and of the temper of the men of letters who cultivated it, by examining a famous civil suit heard by the *conservatori* of the city government in 1519. The suit concerned Christophe de Longueil, a brilliant young French humanist whose career and life were to be ruined by the fanatical Roman literary men into whose hands he fell. Longueil had been born in Flanders in 1488 and had studied at Poitiers. While at the latter city, about 1508, he had distinguished himself by a Latin oration in praise of France and of King Louis XII. In the argument of this oration he had sought to show that the "Gauls" were surpassing the Romans in total achievements. Longueil, known humanistically as Longolius, was a very ambitious young academic, and, after trying unsuccessfully to become a special student of the great Budé in Paris, he decided to go to Rome to learn Greek and to continue his work in Latin. It was not the best choice of a place to study Greek because the local humanists were obsessed with Latinity. They tended to resent the presence of *Graeculi* ("Greeklings") who had come from Constantinople and other cities of the former Byzantine Empire and who failed to be sufficiently impressed by the antiquity of the Eternal City. Pope Leo was, however, very much interested in

Greek studies and founded in Rome a college for Greek boys.

Longolius obtained a position as a tutor and attended classes of the great professor Janus Lascaris, director of the Greek College. He soon gave up the idea of becoming an orator in Greek (having been bested in an exchange of Greek letters with Budé) but managed to become a member of the city's finest literary circles. In 1517 he read five Latin orations in praise of Rome at a private house. One of his well-placed friends asked the *conservatori* to grant him Roman citizenship. (It is not really clear whether this citizenship, soon granted, was a sort of routine naturalization or a coveted distinction given *honoris causa*.) But Longolius was very vain, and he had made some enemies. Several young Romans, perhaps jealous of his oratorical powers in "the Roman tongue," began to arouse opinion against him. They had discovered the youthful oration at Poitiers in which he had exalted the French over the Romans. Celso Mellini and three other young noblemen signed a complaint accusing him of *perduellio*, that is, treason, or, as we may better translate in this case, *lèse-romanité*. On his side Longolius had some very important personages, including Bembo, Sadoleto, and probably Pope Leo. His partisans decided, however, to let the law suit take its course, probably because it promised to offer some first-class entertainment.

Terrible things were told about Longolius. It was asserted that he had been sent to Rome by the northern humanists Erasmus and Budé in order to steal manuscripts. The northern barbarians would have a good laugh at the expense of the Romans when Longolius returned to Paris laden with booty and certified as a *civis romanus*! The *conservatori,* very reluctant to pronounce judgment, invited Roman *letterati* to give evidence on the Campidoglio. An enormous crowd attended the hearing. Longolius' friends were more numerous among the witnesses than were his opponents, the latter being perhaps loath to appear in public against a man who was said to have support in the Vatican. A still more solemn confrontation between Longolius himself and chief accuser Mellini was scheduled. When that day came, Longolius had fled the city, frightened by stones thrown in the street and by a rumor that an assassin had marked him out, but his defense was prepared and could be read by a friend. This time the pope himself and a number of cardinals attended the open hearing. One would have thought that the safety of Rome was at stake. Mellini's oration was elegant and vigorous. He addressed his listeners as *"Quirites,"* just as though they were civic-minded Romans of classical times. Rome had seen many misfortunes since the end of antiquity, he said, but the cynical actions of Longolius constituted an insult without parallel. One should beware of the praises of a barbarian—*Timeo danaos.* Longolius' defense was also magnificently Ciceronian and archaicizing. He endeavored to refute three arguments or charges brought against him:

1. that he had offended the majesty of Rome with the youthful oration in Poitiers,

2. that he was an ignorant and low-born man,

3. that it was unconstitutional to grant Roman citizenship to "Gauls."

In considering this last charge, both he and his opponents assumed that the city had had an unbroken constitutional history since the Age of Cicero. Longolius included in the defense many passages from the earlier orations in praise of Rome and obsequious references to Roman rule of the world.

News of the great trial spread fast. When Longolius arrived in Paris, he was greeted as though he had escaped from madmen. To everyone's surprise, however, he refused to join in denunciations of Rome and stated that he expected to go back. He was infected with the Roman, Ciceronian fever, and it was to take away his health and his life. While in the North he visited Budé and Erasmus but refused an offer of King Francis I to remain as a professor in Paris. He went to Venice, with his eye on Rome. Secretary Sadoleto, acting for Cardinal Giulio dei Medici, the Pope's regent in Florence, offered Longolius the prestigious chair of Latin letters and eloquence in that city; but the young man haughtily refused, apparently feeling that the post was not worthy of him. He settled in Padua, under the protection of the English Cardinal Reginald Pole, and devoted himself to improving still more his Ciceronian style. He put out a new, corrected version of his *Defensiones* (having been in agony lest unauthorized editions contain non-Ciceronian Latin) and, when passions had died down, the Roman *conservatori* finally sent him a diploma of citizenship. He composed a grand oration against Lutheranism, thinking no doubt that he was striking a mighty blow for the unity of Christendom, and then died in 1522, exhausted by his fanatical stylistic studies.

Erasmus speaks a great deal about the case of Longolius in his polemical dialogue the *Ciceronianus* (1528). He finds that the young man had made himself ridiculous by catering to "the emotions of men who dream of ancient Rome . . . just as the Jews dream of their Moses and the temple at Jerusalem." To be a citizen of Rome today, says one of Erasmus' characters, is "something less than to be a citizen of Basel." Longolius is also the model, in the dialogue, for the ridiculous personage Nosoponus, who is ruining his health in devotion to Cicero. Nosoponus no longer allows his eyes to see the words of any other author. He has made alphabetical lexicons of all words and phrases used by Cicero (with separate listings for all inflected noun and verb forms) so that he can check his own sentences for orthodoxy. In his monomania he is no longer of any service either to scholarship or to religion.

The most charming aspects of Roman literary life did not center around the Vatican or the Campidoglio but around private houses and gardens called *orti letterari*. Men of letters were accustomed to meet together for conversation very frequently, much more frequently than now. Anyone who has experienced the peculiar beauty of Roman gardens today can imagine the pleasantness of the setting for literary gatherings in the sixteenth century. The best known of the numerous *orti letterari* in the early sixteenth century were those of Angelo Colocci and Giano Corizio. Colocci was a very learned man in both Greek and Latin, and he had as well a very strong scholarly interest in early vernacular poetry—an interest rather rare among Roman humanists. He wrote Italian *endecasillabi* as well as Latin hexameters. His garden, in the good Roman style, had a fountain (which was celebrated in verse by his friends) and a collection of ancient statuary. Giano Corizio was a native of Luxembourg whose name in German was Johann Küritz. Though he was not so learned a man, he became the most beloved friend of writers in Rome and many verses were written in his honor. He commissioned the sculptor Sansovino to carve for the Church of Sant' Agostino a group of statuary representing the Christ-child, the Virgin Mary, and her mother, Saint Anne. This graceful work is still visible in the church. Saint Anne was Corizio's patron and he invited his friends each year to celebrate her day, first with a ceremony at the church and then in his *orto*. Poets composed verses for the occasion and tacked them up in the church near the statues.

In 1524 a friend of Corizio, Blosio Palladio, published an anthology of poetry dedicated to him. Most or all of it had been written for the feast of Saint Anne in one year or another. This book, called the *Coryciana*, is the major poetic anthology of High Renaissance Rome. One hundred twenty poets, distinguished and mediocre, are represented. The compositions are short, and in many of them the authors have sought an epigrammatic tone based on clever conceits which are no longer much appreciated. Thus the sculptor is praised for his unique accomplishment of drawing three divinities from a single block of marble. There is much innocent neo-paganism. The poet Flaminius asks the "gods" to whom Corizio has dedicated his statue to grant him long life with good wine and, after death, a place at the banquets of the gods with his wine changed to nectar. Printed along with these occasional poems was a poetic treatise by Francesco Arsilli, called *De poetis urbanis*. It is a kind of epigrammatic catalog of Roman poets of the day, with kind words for all. (*Urbanus* is a synonym for *romanus*, since for these proud Romans there could still be only one *urbs*.) The poem begins with a lament on the low state of literary patronage in Rome—a jarring note that puzzled modern scholars until Domenico Gnoli surmised that the first section had been written before the accession of Leo X.

Collective volumes were the rule for published verse in the early sixteenth century, and the inspiration was often occasional, with private as well as public events providing subject matter. Following the accidental death of Celso Mellini—chief enemy of Longolius—there appeared a collection of *lacrimae*, or laments, by his friends.

Almost every year, beginning in 1509, there was published in Rome an anthology of poems called *Pasquinate*, and these annual volumes, along with a few related publications, give us a glance at a more popular, less learned level of literary life than what we have seen heretofore. *Pasquino* was a literary institution in High Renaissance Rome and remained one for a long time afterward. The name belonged to a mutilated ancient statue that had been uncovered in 1501 and set up outside the palace of Cardinal Caraffa. It may still be seen today, on approximately the same site, just off the Piazza Navona. There developed a custom of affixing verses to the statue on the day of Saint Mark, April 25. Each year the statue was dressed up to represent a mythological character or, later, an abstract virtue, and the disguise furnished the theme for the literary compositions. In the first year of Leo's pontificate *Pasquino* appeared as Apollo (modeled after the magnificent Apollo di Belvedere in the Vatican collection), in other years as Mercury, as Orpheus, as Proteus, as Hercules killing Cacus, as a pilgrim, etc.

Anyone could add his verses to the collection hanging around the statue, and in the first years there were apparently many students who took part. The editor of the published volume had sometimes to correct the poets' Latin or to reject their compositions if the Latin was too bad, for most of the verses seem then to have been written in

99

that language, even for posting in the street. In the first few years a preponderance of the poetry was apparently high-minded and conformist in inspiration, though one cannot be sure how many poems of a different nature were rejected by the editor. Starting about 1517, satirical poems became frequent. (And with satire the use of Italian became more common.) It is thought that Pope Leo forbade the observance of the custom in 1519 because of the virulent attacks on the *Curia* posted the year before. Great crowds came to see the poems on Saint Mark's Day and many people brought along pen and ink for copying.

After a while satirical compositions written at other times of the year, and attached to the statue or not, were also called *pasquinate*. (The term spread as well to other parts of Italy and to Germany.) A vast production of *pasquinate* appeared on the death of Pope Leo and during the ensuing conclave to choose his successor, and we may take a few of these as examples of the genre. One poem sarcastically enjoins people to weep: cheap musicians, buffoons, ham actors, gluttonous friars, Florence and its bankers, because the source of their support is cut off. If Pope Leo had lived longer, the poet says, he would have sold out Rome, Christ, and himself. Another poem shows the pope in hell (or, rather, after the neo-pagan style, in the kingdom of the Styx), lamenting because Saint Peter has not allowed him to enter heaven.

Some clever satirist hit upon the idea of designing medals for prominent people, with a Latin motto and, sometimes, a portrait or an emblem. These medals, made probably of plaster or cardboard, were shown around for the delight of the populace. Some of them were indeed very clever. Serapica, secret chamberlain of Pope Leo, was shown with

Accursio, who had held the same office under Julius II. The motto was: "*Sic transit gloria mundi, frater mi.*" For the archpoet Camillo Querno, noted drinker and glutton, it was: "*Virtus mea dereliquit me, et turbata sunt omnia viscera mea*" ("My virtue has left me and all my viscera are thrown into disorder"). Cardinal Trivulzio, an enemy of the Medici, was shown in a pose of melancholy but with the words "Alleluia! Alleluia!" below. The "wife" of Cardinal Grassi was represented (perhaps with him beside her), the following Bible verse being below: "*Benedictus fructus ventris tui*" ("Blessed is the fruit of thy womb"). Numerous cardinals were shown as aspiring vainly to the papacy. The Cardinal of Volterra and Cardinal Giulio dei Medici appeared with the papal tiara between them, the motto being: "*Nec mihi nec tibi*" ("Neither to me nor to you").

The most energetic writer of satirical poetry during the conclave was apparently Pietro Aretino, then only twenty-nine years old and near the beginning of his career as the "scourge of princes" and most successful satirist of the century. He had already gained some reputation in 1516, while a servant of the banker Agostino Chigi, by composing a humorous and biting will for the dead elephant Hanno. During the conclave Aretino posted many sonnets on the statue of Pasquino. While making fun of practically everyone, he was apparently trying to serve the chances of Cardinal Giulio dei Medici (who was to be passed over this time but chosen in 1523). Aretino became known as the chancellor of Master Pasquino, and much of his literary formation came in this early apprenticeship in Rome.

Rome was in sum a very exciting place for men of letters to live. With the official literary activity of the Vatican and the Campidoglio, the good fellowship of the *orti letterari*, and the popular manifestations of Master Pasquino, there was stimulation for literary types as different as pedants and journalists. Both Longolius and Aretino were in their element. It was not a milieu for sober and dedicated geniuses; Dante would have abhorred it. It was probably not the best place for getting serious work done, and Ariosto was doubtless wise, from the professional point of view, to return to Ferrara after paying his respects to the pope in 1512. But in Rome there was not the slightest chance of boredom.

It is inevitable that one should compare the polite and literary society of Rome with that of the little court of Urbino, whose portrait was fixed for posterity in Castiglione's *The Courtier*. The comparison was undoubtedly made at the time, for six of the characters who take part in Castiglione's dialogues (supposedly of 1509) became in the next decade prominent members of Roman society. They were Giuliano dei Medici, Federico Fregoso (later a cardinal), Bernardo Dovizi (a cardinal under Leo X), Bernardo Accolti (nicknamed the *Unico Aretino*), and Pietro Bembo. And one must add to this list of names that of the author himself, who presumably wrote *The Courtier* partly out of nostalgia for Urbino. At first the advantage seems altogether with the smaller city. Refinement of taste appears to have been so much greater there than at the court of Leo X. The archpoets Querno and Baraballo would have been found less amusing in Urbino, and, since there were ladies present, the excesses of pedantry were forbidden. Longolius, the Ciceronian, would have been very gauche and dull as a member of the circle of Urbino. The scandal-mongering Aretino would also have been unwelcome, for different reasons. But Roman society was vast and cosmopolitan with extremes of all sorts and cannot be judged with the same standards of a small, elite court. Between the extremes there was room for private circles of every kind. The most refined of the *orti letterari* would, but for the absence of ladies and the cult of Latin, have borne comparison with Urbino. And we may assume that Bembo and Castiglione, by choosing their friends carefully, were able to find the sort of company they preferred.

What of the part of artists in the intellectual society of Rome? Not a great deal is known about it since artists did not write much about their own lives and their names appear less frequently than those of writers in contemporary accounts. In the High Renaissance, when great art was appreciated as in few times of history, surprisingly little attention was sometimes paid to the identity of artists. It is probable that they did not often move in the same circles with writers in Rome and that this separation was largely a result of the fact that artists did not know Latin. They would not have appreciated classical orations and would even have been bored by much of the entertainment at the *orti letterari*.

The case of Raphael is exceptional. Though he was also without much Latin and had to ask a friend to explain to him the architectural treatise of Vitruvius, his company was prized by literary men, and it may be said that he belonged to their world. He was the most admired artist in the city and, unlike Michelangelo (who would later have an even greater reputation for artistic genius and would even become quite a good poet in Italian), he had the advantage of an easygoing nature and a personal charm that made him beloved by people of all kinds. He lived

handsomely in a town house near the Vatican and much
enjoyed social occasions. There is a record of an excursion
to examine the ruins of Hadrian's villa at Tivoli that he
made in the company of Bembo, Castiglione, Cardinal
Bibbiena, and other writers. One imagines that the conversation on this occasion must have been quite up to the
standards of Urbino!

Raphael died in 1519, aged only thirty-seven, the victim,
his friends thought, of excessive indulgence in the lighter
pleasures. His death brought personal grief to an extraordinary number of people. A typical reaction is found in
the following letter of a Venetian correspondent, which
because of its information on Raphael's standing and other
matters we shall reproduce at length:

"On Holy Friday, at night, toward Saturday morning,
at three A.M., died the most polite and excellent painter
Raphael of Urbino, with the universal grief of all and especially of the learned . . . and also of painters and architects.
He was setting forth in a book, as Ptolemy set forth the
world, the ancient buildings of Rome, showing so clearly
their proportions, forms, and ornaments that seeing it
would have been as good for anyone as seeing ancient
Rome. And he had already finished the first region. He not
only showed the plans and the site of the buildings . . .
but also drew the façades with their ornaments, as he had
learned about them from Vitruvius and from architectural
theory and from ancient historians (if the ruins no longer
showed them). Now death has interrupted such a beautiful and praiseworthy enterprise, having stolen away the
master only thirty-four years old [sic], and on his very
birthday."

"The pontiff himself suffered great sorrow . . . and in the

fifteen days he was sick sent people to visit and to comfort him quite six times. Imagine what other people must have done. . . . every gentle spirit must sorrow and grieve not only with simple and temporary voices, but also with careful and perpetual [literary] compositions, as, if I'm not wrong, these writers are preparing to do in abundance. It is said that he left 16,000 [*ducati*], including 5,000 in cash, to be divided for the most part among his friends and servants; and the house, which used to belong to Bramante, which he bought for 3,000 *ducati*, he left to the Cardinal of Santa Maria in Portico [Bibbiena]. And he was buried in the Rotonda [Pantheon], to which he was borne with all honor. His soul has doubtless gone to contemplate those heavenly [artistic] workshops that allow no competition, but his name will remain down here on earth and in the thought and minds of right-thinking people for a long time."

The letter writer goes on to report the death of the great banker, Agostino Chigi, whom he thought to have left 800,000 *ducati*. He has the good sense to say that this death has done "much less harm" to the world than that of the beloved young artist.

FAITH AND MORALS

I N APRIL, 1520, Martin Luther attached to his treatise on Christian liberty a public letter to Pope Leo X which contained the following remarkable passage: "I must . . . acknowledge my total abhorrence of your see, the Roman court, which neither you nor any man can deny is more corrupt than either Babylon or Sodom, and, according to the best of my information, is sunk in the most deplorable and notorious impiety."

Luther professed still a personal reverence of the pope, who had the misfortune to be surrounded by evil men: "In the meantime, you, o Leo, sit like a lamb amidst wolves, and live like Daniel amidst the lions, or Ezekiel among the scorpions. But what can you oppose to these monsters? Three or four learned and excellent cardinals. . . . The fate of the court of Rome is decreed; the wrath of God is upon it. . . . Under these impressions, I have always lamented, o most excellent Leo, that you, who are worthy of better times, should have been elected to the pontificate in such days as these. Rome merits you not."

By this time the vision of Rome as a new Babylon was common in northern Europe and frequently evoked in Italy as well. The later progress of the Protestant Reformation naturally favored the propagation of the idea, and with the Counter-Reformation Catholics in turn looked back on the time of Leo X with misgivings. To what extent is the Roman reputation for impiety and wickedness deserved? No sure answer can be given to questions involving the private faith and morals of fifty thousand people, but we can examine some indications of the spirit of the time.

The question of religious faith can be disposed of, if not quite settled, very quickly. Luther, who had spent a month in Rome in 1510–11, thought that there were many atheists in the city and in Italy and that educated people remarked openly that they went to mass only "to conform to the popular error." There is virtually no evidence to support such an idea. If non-believers were common, they hid their ideas remarkably well. Moreover, the Roman people were exceedingly fond of religious ceremonies, and the popes and most cardinals seem to have been very diligent in carrying out their priestly duties. The theory of a cynical and free-thinking Rome exploiting the credulity of the rest of Christendom must be allowed to fall for lack of evidence. Whatever its faults, Rome was a Christian city.

Leaving the domain of faith for that of morals, we find much evidence to support the charge of corruption. One great scandal of Pope Leo's time revealed the seamy side of life at the Vatican court to all of Europe. This was the Conspiracy of the Cardinals, denounced to the world in 1517. Though the discovery of the plot was given great publicity at the time, the Church soon wished to forget it. Efforts to push the affair into oblivion were so successful that modern historians until recently had grave doubts about it. Some, echoing anti-Medici rumors of the period, suggested that the conspiracy had never existed at all but had been trumped up for political reasons by the pope and his advisers. The Italian scholar Fabrizio Winspeare has, however, demonstrated that the conspiracy was real, if somewhat vague and naïve. Permitted to use documents in the Vatican Archives, he has uncovered enough information to reconstruct the essential sequence of events. The following account is based mainly on his book *La Congiura dei Cardinali contro Leone X.*

The background of this ecclesiastical plot was not unlike that of plots in secular courts. Some of the cardinals were very rich and powerful men, and all knew that they were in theory eligible to be elected pope themselves one day. The main villain in the conspiracy was Cardinal Alfonso Petrucci, a *bon vivant* in his early twenties who had been one of the main supporters of Giovanni dei Medici in the conclave. His change of view arose from personal grievances, the most important of these being the pope's support of another Petrucci in a seizure of the lordship of Siena from the cardinal's brother. Three other cardinals seem to have been involved in the plot as well, though their guilt is nothing like so clear as that of Petrucci. They were Bandinello Sauli, another young prelate; Francesco Soderini, brother of the Piero Soderini who had been deposed as head of Florence's republican government on the return of the Medici; and the wealthy Raffaele Riario, an older man who had been a candidate for the papal tiara in 1512 and who still held ambitions. It is possible that some important people outside the Church were also involved: Francesco Maria della Rovere, who had lost his dukedom of Urbino to the pope's nephew Lorenzo; some representatives of the Spanish government; and some members of the Colonna family.

The basic facts of the conspiracy are simple. It was planned to have Pope Leo murdered by a doctor who would administer poison through an ulcer on the pope's buttock. The doctor was Giovan Battista da Vercelli, a man famous both for his medical talents and for his violence, whom it was hoped Leo would engage as his personal physician. The pontiff did not hire Vercelli and the plot, perhaps never completely worked out, came to naught long before it was discovered. Petrucci had, however, continued to machinate against the pope, and some of his associates were arrested in April, 1517. It was principally through the interrogation of the cardinal's servant, Marc Antonio Nini, that the facts of the failed plot came to light. The entire testimony of Nini has survived, having been taken down in Latin as he spoke in Italian. He was held and questioned in the Castel Sant' Angelo, main fortress and prison of the city. He was a naturally garrulous fellow who revealed more than he intended on many occasions, but his confession was owed principally to his being subjected to torture. Our blood is chilled by the matter-of-fact tone of the clerk describing the torture and interrogation, for if torture exists today, it is not often practiced openly and without any qualms of conscience. In the Renaissance, as long before and afterward, most people seem to have thought it proper to make guilty men confess through torture. They apparently assumed that the innocent would find some means, human or divine, of resisting. On one day the record states that *after having been taken down from the rack* Nini began to speak "of his own free will" (*sua sponte*). Winspeare points out that this "of his own free will" is horribly revealing of the judicial philosophy of the period.

Leo X, informed of Nini's revelations, lured Cardinal Petrucci back to Rome from a castle of the Colonnas where he had been staying. The pope pretended to have changed his mind in regard to the pretensions of Petrucci to the signory of Siena and asked Cardinals Sauli and Cornaro to help effect a reconciliation. A detailed agreement was drawn up promising the cardinal recovery of Siena in return for loyalty to the Holy See. On May 17, the cardinal signed it at Genazzano. Leo X then sent him a safe-conduct to Rome, guaranteeing that he would not be punished for past political transgressions. The crime of conspiracy to murder was not covered. The cardinal arrived happily in Rome on the evening of May 18. The next morning he proceeded grandly to the Vatican, with a large retinue. Cardinals Sauli and Cornaro, who had acted in good faith, were waiting to receive him in the pope's antechamber. When only a few words had been exchanged among the three, a captain of the guards entered with some of his men. He blocked all exits, seized Cardinals Petrucci and Sauli and took them to the dungeons of Sant' Angelo. Cardinal Cornaro was left free, though greatly frightened.

That same morning a consistory of the remaining cardinals in Rome was held. Leo X informed them of the arrests and of the main facts uncovered about the conspiracy. With unusual energy in his manner, he announced his intention of pushing the investigation to its end and of seeing that guilty persons were punished. All the cardinals, with or without guilty consciences, were horribly upset. So, soon, was the whole city of Rome.

Pietro Bembo and Jacopo Sadoleto, the pope's erudite Latin secretaries, set to work immediately on letters to foreign heads of state and to nuncios in foreign capitals to inform them of the plot and the arrests. Foreign ambassadors in Rome were also convoked and informed. The next day, when the Venetian ambassador (who had been absent) called at the Vatican, he found it teeming with guards and had to get special permission to enter. The pope took all military precautions and remained securely in his apartments without going out for over a month.

The physician Vercelli was arrested in Florence on May 19 and put on the way to Rome. Lesser personages in Rome were seized and put into prison. The city thrilled with alarm and curiosity. The political atmosphere was not unlike that which had prevailed under Nero and other insecure ancient emperors. It was rumored that the imprisoned cardinals were being tortured. That was probably untrue, although the pope had ordered his investigators to proceed quickly, by all means, and with no respect of persons.

When the cardinals met again on the morning of May 29, the pope kept them waiting as he consulted in a private room with Cardinal Accolti. At length the Cardinals Farnese and Riario were ushered into the room, smiling. Riario was immediately surrounded by guards, and the pope left the room, ordering that the consistory be adjourned. Later that day he informed the Holy College that the venerable cardinal had been arrested because the other accused had implicated him in their plot. Riario, then about seventy years old, was at first held in an apartment of the Vatican, with servants to attend to him. Learned, rich, and generous, this cardinal seems to have had many friends among both the powerful and the common people of Rome, and his arrest was much resented. Military forces were increased to prevent a possible popular uprising. On June 4, Riario was moved to Castel Sant' Angelo, apparently because he had tried to take back some earlier confessions. On hearing that he was to be taken to the dungeons, the old man fainted. When he came back to his senses, he was so weak that he had to be carried on a litter through the passage running over the walls to the ancient fortress.

At another consistory called on June 8, the pope electrified his cardinals once again by telling them he knew two more of their number were guilty. He was ready to pardon these men, after the example of Christ, if they would come forward and beg forgiveness. It was suggested from the floor that the guilty be allowed to confess without revealing themselves to the others. Each cardinal was to file by and kiss the pontiff; the guilty would whisper their confessions in his ear. When, however, Cardinal Soderini passed with only the ritual words "Pax tibi," Leo stopped him and made an open accusation. After some argument Soderini and Cardinal Castellesi knelt weeping at the pope's feet. He then dramatically granted his Christian pardon, requiring only that they conduct themselves well in the future—and pay fines of 12,500 ducati. Everyone was much moved by this scene, which seemed to hark back to the days of primitive Christianity. The confessions of the two were not to be made known outside the Holy College, but naturally the news leaked out. (Minio, the Venetian ambassador, could not rest until he had found what had transpired.) The two cardinals both fled into exile after a few days, fearing less, perhaps, a breach of faith on the part of their master than the vengefulness of his followers.

On June 22, Cardinals Petrucci, Sauli, and Riario were sentenced to degradation from their rank, confiscation of property, and—most frighteningly—release into the hands of *secular* justice. That very evening, in prison, the three men were stripped of their marks of office.

On June 27, Nini and the physician Vercelli were executed publicly and with great cruelty. They were first paraded through the city on a cart which was preceded by the city executioner and other officers on foot. On the cart with them were an officer of justice and a hot brazier of coals. The officer periodically took from the brazier a pair of red-hot pincers and ripped off a piece of flesh from one of the condemned men. The mob, made bestial by such a spectacle, covered the screams of the tortured criminals with their own yells. When the procession had arrived at the Piazza del Ponte, the two men were hanged, Vercelli loudly protesting his innocence till the end. He may indeed never have intended to kill the pope, though he had certainly not rejected the suggestion outright. The bodies of the two men were later taken down from the gallows, drawn and quartered, and hung up again. It was customary everywhere to stage particularly horrible executions for regicides.

About a week later former Cardinal Petrucci was executed privately in Castel Sant' Angelo. He was strangled with a crimson silk noose by a Moorish executioner (it being considered improper for a Christian to do harm to a former prince of the Church). Petrucci is supposed to have rejected a chance to implore God's mercy on his soul, exclaiming, "Since it is destined that I should lose my body, I do not care at all about losing my soul!" He seems to have been one of the few genuine atheists of the time.

Sentiment and pressure had been growing for the pardon of the two cardinals still in prison, especially Riario. The fanatical members of the Medici party in Florence wanted them to be killed, but other cardinals, prominent Roman citizens, and Italian and foreign princes interceded. Pardon of the two men would plainly be a wise political move and the interest of the Church would be served. Pardon would also be profitable, since Riario could offer a large sum as fine. The release of Riario was decided first. It had severe conditions, including a public confession before the consistory, an oath of absolute obedience, and the presentation of the vast sum of 150,000 *ducati* in three installments. The payment of the fine was guaranteed in advance by other people. The principal guarantor was the great Roman banker Agostino Chigi, and other prominent names were on the list. Cardinal Riario must really have been one of the most beloved men in Rome. He was released on July 27. The news of his impending pardon had spread through the city, and there was a happy crowd in the streets below when he walked back through the covered passage from Sant' Angelo to the Vatican Palace. He entered the solemn consistory, knelt before the pontiff, and kissed his foot. Leo X then raised him up and kissed him on the cheek. Riario made an emotional confession, saying he was even more guilty than his written avowals made it appear. The pope treated him with ostentatious kindness. Cardinal Sauli was pardoned soon afterward. Because of his limited means, he had to pay only 25,000 *ducati*.

Thus ended the main events of the Conspiracy of the

Cardinals, which had shaken pontifical Rome to its foundations and was for months the talk of Europe. What does the plot tell us about the moral condition of the Roman court? Petrucci was an odious character, and though the intention to murder of the other accused cardinals is not certain, there can be no doubt that they were enemies of their pope. These princes of the Church retained powerful worldly ambitions and sometimes behaved in the same way as unscrupulous politicians in secular states. It is not at all sure, however, that a majority of the cardinals of the time were of this sort, and one should remember as well that even the worldliest of them could be pious and kind in certain contexts. The conspiracy was not evidence of total corruption. And modern readers are almost as much revolted by the violence of judicial questioning and punishment as by the venality and treason of the guilty cardinals.

It was thought in anti-Roman circles of Northern Europe that cardinals lived lives of open dissipation in the company of courtesans and rakes. This idea was certainly exaggerated, but there can be no doubt that cardinals of the time were much less austere than those of today. They attended parties and gave them much in the manner of other wealthy people of the city. The Venetian correspondent Tomà Lippomano sent home an account of one very interesting party given for cardinals during the carnival season of 1519. It was the sort of thing that would have shocked Luther but aroused the admiration of the worldly correspondent.

"I don't want to miss telling you about a party the banker Lorenzo Strozzi, brother-in-law of Duke Lorenzo of Urbino, gave to four most reverend Cardinals, that is, Rossi, Cibò, Salviati, and Ridolfi, all nephews and cousins of the Pope, and certain other Florentines who were buffoons and three whores. It was one of the finest parties that have been given in Rome, but a frightful thing and one which did not please the Cardinals. When they entered the said Strozzi's house, they were led around . . . till they came to a black door [and] once the door was raised they entered into a room covered in black . . . and full of skulls, and in the four corners of the said salon were painted four Deaths very ugly and frightful, with a little candle behind them that caused great fear. In the middle of the salon was a table also covered with black, with a wooden dish in the middle holding two skulls with four dead men's bones and four wooden cups full of wine. The host said: 'Gentlemen, have a snack, and we will go to supper later.' No one would eat because it was a frightful thing, and when the skulls were broken open, there were cooked pheasants inside, and sausages inside the bones. And one fellow called Fra Mariano, who is the buffoon of the Pope, said to Brandino, who . . . is called Cordiale by everybody here, Fra Mariano said to him: 'Cordial *mio*, what have we got into? I don't want this to be a total loss,' and they began to eat a bite and to drink a glass of wine. Then they left that place and entered a big room that seemed to be a very beautiful starry world, with very many lights . . . and they sat down at table. They were fourteen in all. As soon as they had sat down . . . there rose up fourteen dishes of salad . . . one for each. Then they asked for something to drink, and fourteen glasses of wine were brought, and one didn't know where they came from, if not from under the room. Then came pheasants and partridges in quantity, and when they were busy eating, there was a great explosion and the world [things] started to move around and where there had been pheasants came other things that were not good, and the lights went out. At this moment there came two men, one dressed as Fra Mariano and the other as Brandino, and said: 'I am Fra Mariano who wants to eat some more,' and the same for Brandino. And the real Fra Mariano, who was there at table, seeing these men, said: 'Cordial *mio*, here we are, I don't know who those fellows are.' And then the world [things] stopped moving, and the two dressed as Fra Mariano and Brandino went away, and the Cardinals began to vomit, and the others too except for three or four, and one of those whores among the leading ones of Rome called 'Mama doesn't want me to.' And immediately there came other dishes of different things, but the Cardinals wouldn't stay at table any more and got up and went away, not a third of the supper having been finished. And so this supper is held to be one of the finest ever given in Rome, and a lot of money was spent for it, but everyone was very much frightened. I should have liked to be there to see it, even if it had cost me a pair of *ducati*."

The evening may seem to us just an ingeniously planned, Halloween-type party, and there is nothing shocking except the presence of the courtesans. Ladies of their profession were apparently unusually plentiful in Rome, where a large celibate population and the flow of travelers assured them a large clientele. *Madrema non vuole*, or "Mama doesn't want me to," who was present at this party —and whom we have already seen as a linguistic purist— belonged to the highest stratum of her trade. She and her most fortunate sisters had a status somewhat like that of the best Japanese geishas, since they were esteemed as often for their company and conversation as for their physical attractions. (There is no reason to think that Madrema had any other duty besides that of conversation at the party.) The greatest of the courtesans had been Imperia, who flourished in the pontificate of Julius II. Her beauty and charm were famous. She counted cardinals and the banker Agostino Chigi among her admirers, though not, perhaps, among her lovers. Her apartment was so magnificent that the Spanish ambassador, on a visit, was reported to have spit into the face of his own servant because it was the only non-precious object in the room. Imperia had a tragic and romantic end in 1512, at only thirty years old, when she poisoned herself because of a hopeless love for a married man. She died in Christian penitence.

Pietro Aretino, who lived in Rome during the time of Popes Leo and Clement, delighted later in depicting the low life of the city, particularly the life of prostitutes. In his scabrous *Ragionamenti*, a wise and witty old courtesan named Nanna gives advice to a pretty young apprentice on how to rise to the top of the profession. She talks a great deal about good manners and also tells the girl to keep some fashionable pieces of literature, such as Ariosto's *Orlando furioso* and Petrarch's poems, on her table so that her suitors will think she is reading them. Nanna herself, in her best days, had been more than a common prostitute. She had played favorites among her lovers, and not every man with the minimum fee was admitted to her bed. She had not, indeed, thought in terms of fees at all but had aimed at being supported in style and at receiving luxurious gifts that would allow her to cut a good figure among her sisters. There was apparently much consciousness of social standing among the more successful of them.

Alvigia, another retired courtesan portrayed by Aretino, in his play *La Cortegiana*, reminisces fondly about the days of her youth when she had been one of the most successful members of her profession: "Now, to tell you the truth . . . I can say 'To Hell with the world!' since I have been able to indulge so many of my whims. In my day neither Ancioletta da Napoli, nor Beatrice, nor *Madrema non vuole*, nor that great Imperia was fit to lace my shoes. Fashions, masks, fine houses, bull fighting, horse riding, sables trimmed in gold, parrots, monkeys, and numbers of maids and servants were nothing to me. And signori and monsignori and ambassadors aplenty."

These brief recollections give us a glimpse of what the *dolce vita* must have been like for prosperous members of the Roman *demi monde*. Alvigia had delighted in the appearance of wealth and in showing herself off in public, and one can imagine her going through the streets of Rome in her best finery, accompanied by servants, and looking haughtily at the people along her way. (One can imagine also the pursed lips of virtuous matrons who saw her pass.) Her choice of pets—parrots and monkeys—shows a taste for the appearance of luxury since these animals were exotic and costly. They must have made a terrific racket in her house, but Alvigia was not the contemplative type and, like most Italians even today, could probably endure an extraordinary amount of noise.

Many of the courtesans' customers were tourists or pilgrims. Nanna remarks: "Those who come to see Rome want, once they have seen the ancient things, to see also some modern ones, that is, the ladies, and to act with them as gentlemen do." The tourists who fell into Nanna's hands were unfortunate, since she was accustomed to steal their clothes—a more costly possession than today—by a six-teenth-century version of a confidence game. Shortly before a visitor was to leave her place of business, Nanna's maid would come to take his clothes and clean them. Soon afterward, the maid would scream that the clothes had been stolen while her back was turned. When the customer complained to Nanna, several strong bullies would rush up from below to "defend" the lady. The victim was then happy to be allowed to send for more clothes from his lodgings. And Nanna had a thousand other tricks as well. One would think, indeed, from reading Aretino, that most Romans were shysters and thieves lying in wait for newcomers. Maco, the Sienese protagonist of his comedy *La Cortegiana*, is hoodwinked by an extraordinary collection of Roman tricksters. At the very beginning of the play, Rome is termed *coda mundi*, "tail of the world," in a fierce deformation of the classical phrase *caput mundi*, "head of the world." But it must be remembered that Aretino wrote to entertain and virtually without moral purpose.

Sexual promiscuity in the High Renaissance was made dangerous by a new disease—syphilis. The long-held view that the malady had been brought by sailors from America is now disputed, but there can be no doubt that it was new in the early sixteenth century and that it was much more deadly than now both because people did not understand it and because little resistance had been built up. References to the disease—called *il mal francese*, or "French Disease," in Italy—are extremely frequent in the writings of the period. Our friend Alvigia's career had been ruined by it: "And then I contracted a sickness whose name was never discovered, and we treated it as French Disease. And I became old from taking so many medicines and started to rent out rooms, selling rings, dresses, and all the things of my youth. Then I was reduced to taking in embroidered shirts to wash. Then I gave myself over to advising young girls."

A number of famous people, including Lorenzo, Duke of Urbino and Pope Leo's nephew, are thought to have died from the disease. It received its present name from Girolamo Fracastoro, a physician and poet living in Verona during the time. In a long poem of Latin hexameters entitled *Syphilis, sive de morbo gallico*, Fracastoro invented a mythological origin both for the disease and for its treatment with mercury, already known. The young shepherd Syphilis is infected as a punishment for not worshiping Apollo, and the cure is revealed in a similarly supernatural way. This poem, which contains a great deal of natural philosophy as well as literary episodes, is a remarkable example of the fusion of classical learning and science in the Renaissance. It is dedicated to Bembo, Pope Leo's secretary.

Syphilis was treated as well in the *stufe*, great public hot baths that were apparently a recent German importation rather than an inheritance from ancient Rome. The *stufe* were also places of rendezvous and were probably sometimes connected with houses of prostitution. They were, in any case, places of ill fame. The austere Pope Adrian VI, who reigned briefly after Leo X, hurled a terrible insult at Michelangelo's painting of the ceilings of the Sistine Chapel by saying the artist had turned the holy place into a "*stufa* of nudes." The proprietors of *stufe*, often German, would have to mend their ways somewhat with the coming of the Counter-Reformation.

An old native Roman like Marc Antonio Altieri might

have argued that the corruption and immorality existing in the city were due to the influx of foreigners. He would have been on very weak ground so far as political venality and violence were concerned, for the old families of the Orsini and the Colonna needed no lessons from anybody in that field. In regard to private and sexual immorality his protest would have been closer to the truth. Roman matrons were in fact famous for their virtue, and, if we are to believe indications from works of fiction, many prostitutes and their shady associates do seem to have come from elsewhere. It was quite natural that a dynamic city where money was flowing and visitors were numerous should attract persons of questionable character. Natural, but unfortunate when the city in question was the spiritual capital of Christendom.

A fascinating and impossible question poses itself. Were the immorality, the venality, and even the violence of the age inseparable from its beauties? Would the same gracefulness of courtly life and the same artistic masterpieces have been possible in a more civic-minded and more puritanical society? Historians no longer try to answer such questions, and the answers of philosophers are contradictory.

EPILOGUE: A PURITAN, ANOTHER MEDICI, AND THE SACK OF ROME

WITHIN SIX YEARS of Pope Leo's death, the city of Rome underwent terrible experiences that encouraged men to look back on his pontificate as a golden age. Harder times set in immediately, for the interregnum was long and uneasy. The College of Cardinals' power to govern the city was weakened by common knowledge that the treasury was empty. It was necessary to mortgage sacred *objets d'art* even to get money for Leo's funeral. The Swiss Guards demanded their backpay, and other servants of the Vatican became restless. The city government of the Campidoglio, asserting itself once again, asked for lower taxes and more authority. Banks closed their doors; merchants refused credit. The public safety was not sure, and people who could, fortified their own houses.

The conclave to choose a new pope did not begin until December 27, nearly four weeks after Leo's death. The people in the streets, also braver in the absence of a pontiff, hissed the cardinals as they passed on their way to the Sistine Chapel. Cardinals Giulio dei Medici and Alessandro Farnese were the strongest candidates. When, however, it became clear that no strong contender could be elected, Medici surprised his colleagues by putting forward the name of an absent cardinal, Adrian of Utrecht, to whom no one would have given a chance. In their fatigue and discouragement the electors voted for him, and the choice was announced from the window in the traditional manner on January 9, 1522.

The Roman people burst into demonstrations of fury and outrage. Adrian was a foreigner! How could a *Tedesco* ["a German"] be bishop of Rome? (It was not the point that Romans and other Italians held church offices in other parts of Europe.) Cardinals were insulted in public because of their action; vicious writings appeared on walls. Outside the Vatican someone posted a Latin notice: *Locanda est*, "for rent." People were anxious as well because Adrian was away in Spain and could not arrive for some time. The near anarchical conditions in the city would thus be prolonged, at best.

Adrian was in fact a Dutchman who had been made a cardinal by Leo X himself in the great nomination of 1517. He had been the tutor of Charles V and was now that sovereign's regent in Spain (where the cantankerous Spanish grandees were making his duties hard to perform). The Imperial party were delighted at his election, though it was to turn out that he had no intention of being a pawn of his former pupil. He received the news of his election in Spain on January 24. It was only with some difficulty that he was persuaded that the news was true, and even then the new pope showed no signs of jubilation. He seemed almost to be considering a refusal of the election, but his sense of duty prevailed, and in mid-February he sent letters of acceptance to the Holy College and to the city fathers of the Campidoglio. A large and disparate fleet carrying the pope to Italy finally set sail from Tarragona on August 5. After stopovers in several ports, it arrived at Ostia on August 28.

Rome had been without a pope for nearly nine months. The city's economic life had been seriously affected, and for some time there had also been a renewal of the plague, so that many wealthy residents had fled to the country. Hospitals were overcrowded, and the crime rate was high. Civic leaders were thus very anxious for the new pope to arrive and take charge, outlander though he was. Adrian VI (who had further disturbed opinion by keeping his baptismal name) proceeded first from Ostia to the Roman church of Saint Paul-outside-the-walls. There, on August 29, he accepted the homage of his cardinals. He showed impatience with the interminable Latin orations they delivered and received coldly the first requests for favors.

It soon became clear that thrift was to be one of Adrian's master qualities. Though the treasury was empty, the Romans were shocked by the new austerity. Several cardinals who had been living luxuriously in the palace were told to find their own accommodations elsewhere, and the pope even spoke of going to live in a smaller house himself because the Vatican cost too much to run. Adrian was bent as well on moral reform. On September 3, he told the cardinals that all of Europe was talking about the corruption of the Roman court and that he intended to make changes.

The heart went out of the public literary and artistic activities. There could be no question of subsidizing poets, and the pope seems to have cut off funds from all artistic projects except, perhaps, Saint Peter's. The literary men of Rome soon began to make their unhappiness known.

The satires of *Pasquino* became so fierce that the pope forbade the customs of covering the statue with verses on Saint Mark's Day. There was an apochryphal story that he had ordered Pasquino to be put in prison, thinking that it was a real man.

In the event, Adrian was no more successful than Leo had been at stopping the Lutheran movement or in getting Christian sovereigns to abandon their costly rivalries. In 1524 he himself was reluctantly drawn into a coalition with the emperor against Francis I. On September 14 of that year he died after a short illness, not having had the power or the time to accomplish his high and difficult purposes. The Roman people predictably burst into expressions of joy on hearing of his illness and death. Someone posted a tasteless inscription on the door of his physician: *Liberatori patriae SPQR*, "From the Roman People and Senate to the Liberator of his Homeland." Even to our own day there has never been another non-Italian pope.

It was again urgent to choose a new pope quickly. The cardinals were not, however, disposed to come to an agreement and this conclave, beginning on October 1, was one of the longest in history. At last an agreement was reached. By threatening to vote for Cardinal Orsini, Giulio dei Medici frightened Cardinal Colonna into throwing support to himself. Medici was elected by acclamation on November 19.

The city showed all signs of joy. Everyone hoped that the new Medici pope, who took the name of Clement VII, would spend money freely as Leo had done. He did not in fact do so because the treasury was low and he had a greater sense of financial responsibility than his cousin. He was not able to give much advancement to the work on

Saint Peter's, which would not proceed rapidly until the time of Paul III. As for literary men, Clement not only gave them less money than Leo had done; he also had much less personal contact with them. The climate in Rome was nevertheless favorable to literature, and there were a number of *orti letterari* and salons. Some of the prominent writers under Leo X had departed, while others remained. Pietro Bembo, Latin secretary, had left after the death of his master. Jacopo Sadoleto, the other secretary, had been obliged in the reforming pontificate of Adrian to go reside in his diocese of Carpentras, but he returned to the *urbs* for a few years after the accession of Clement. Castiglione was sent by the pope as his nuncio to the emperor. His immortal *The Courtier* was published in Clement's time. Aretino, who had made his reputation as a satirist during the conclave for electing Adrian, returned to Rome under Clement and stayed there until 1525, when he was expelled for scurrilous writings against the pope and his datary Giberti. (The writer had become enraged after being stabbed by a rival in love, one of Giberti's household, and seeing the man go unpunished.) Another talented satirist and an excellent poet in Italian, Francesco Berni, lived in Rome and worked for Aretino's enemy Giberti. Vernacular literature was beginning to have better standing in the city, as the Latinist prejudice of Leo's time weakened.

The principal motives of Clement's foreign policy were to be the same as those which had inspired the policy of Leo. He wished to maintain a balance of power in Europe, and he was even more eager than his cousin had been to get the Christian princes to leave off their fighting with each other and unite in a powerful campaign against the

Turks. Clement maneuvered badly, and catastrophe came in 1527. To say that he was responsible for the Sack of Rome is, however, only a little more reasonable than to say that Neville Chamberlain was responsible for World War II. The two men might have avoided disaster by being cleverer, but the criminal responsibility is not theirs.

The series of military and diplomatic events leading to the catastrophe are particularly complex, the enterprises of diplomacy and strategy being confused even more than usual by the slowness of communication. We can examine only the most salient events, with special attention to their effect in the city of Rome. The dominant fact of European politics was still the rivalry between Charles V and Francis I, with Henry VIII beginning to exercise a good deal of influence on the periphery. In Rome, the Colonna party, allied with the emperor, became more obstreperous, and its leader Cardinal Pompeo Colonna worked more or less openly against the pope. Clement had the misfortune to conclude an alliance with Francis I two months before that monarch was taken prisoner by the Spaniards after a terrible defeat at Pavia (February 14, 1525). The pope hastily changed sides, but in May, 1526, when the liberated French king formed another coalition against the emperor, he joined in again. After bad news came from other parts of Italy, however, and the Colonnas rattled their sabers at home, the frightened pontiff reversed himself still again and made an agreement with Ugo de Moncada, ambassador of the emperor. All this vacillation detracted greatly from the dignity of the head of the Church.

On September 20, Cardinal Pompeo Colonna, joined by Moncada, treacherously led a large military force into Rome and tried to rouse the Roman people to rebellion against the pope. The time was favorable for a Ghibelline appeal because of heavy taxes and inflation. There was no general rebellion, but the populace did little to defend their sovereign. The Colonna soldiers erupted into the Borgo quarter of the Vatican and then into the palace itself. The pope, who had first wanted to await the invaders on his throne in pontifical robes, was prevailed upon to go to the fortress of Sant' Angelo through a covered passageway which came in handy at perilous moments. Both the Vatican Palace and Saint Peter's were looted, sacred objects being hauled away for sale. Tapestries designed by Raphael were taken from the Sistine Chapel. Moncada was brought to the castle to negotiate. He was kind enough to bring along with him the pope's tiara, which had been stolen. Clement agreed to various demands, but Pompeo Colonna was not allowed to seize the papacy, as he may have expected, and his bands retired to the hills. Once the crisis was past, the pope turned his mind to revenge. He hired a large number of mercenaries, who succeeded in devastating the country possessions of the Colonnas.

In the north of Italy events were preparing the larger disaster to come. The duke of Bourbon, in the service of Charles, commanded a large army in Lombardy. In the fall of 1526, Baron Frundsberg crossed the Alps from Germany with around twelve thousand mercenaries—called by the Italians *lanzichenecchi*, from the German *Landesknecht*. Giovanni dei Medici, greatest Italian general of the age and father of the future Duke Cosimo I of Florence, died trying to prevent the descent of these men into Italy. The *lanzichenecchi* joined Bourbon's army early in the new year.

Clement considered that he was no longer at war with Spain and the Empire, and he foolishly disbanded again most of his forces. The diplomatic situation was now extremely confused. Charles V was in Spain, about six weeks away for the purpose of sending messages and receiving answers. He was far from up to date on what was happening in Italy and was preoccupied by the terrible news that the king of Hungary had been defeated and killed in battle by the Turks. The kings of France and England were also ill informed and too far away, in any case, to intervene quickly in the affairs of the peninsula. The next course of events was to be determined without the close participation of any of these sovereigns.

The Imperial armies in the north had been moving south. In the middle of March an Imperial legate arrived at Bourbon's camp near Bologna with news of the peace concluded between Clement and Naples. He brought as well thirty thousand *ducati* of tribute given by the Florentines, who feared for the safety of their own city. Bourbon was willing to agree to the peace and turn back north, but his soldiers had their minds set on the booty of Rome and they rebelled. So also did those of Frundsberg, who suffered an attack of apoplexy on seeing the force of the mutiny. His men joined the army of Bourbon, who agreed to lead the entire host southward. There were still two Italian armies that might have stopped them—one nominally in the papal service but commanded by the anti-Medici Duke of Urbino and another, belonging to Florence, under the control of Guicciardini. Neither sought battle with the enemy. At the end of March Bourbon's hordes started across the Apennines, sacking small towns along the way. When further efforts to bribe Bourbon and his soldiers to turn back failed, Clement at last understood his peril and began to move with energy. He summoned the ambassadors of France, England, Venice, and Milan and announced that he was again their ally against Spain. He promised to excommunicate the emperor and absolve his subjects from the duty of obedience. Serious efforts were made to prepare the city's defenses.

The Romans manned the walls to await the attack. It began before dawn on the morning of May 6, with *lanzichenecchi* assaulting the walls nearest the Vatican. The defenders threw down boiling water, hot pitch, and torches. Many attackers died in the first phase of battle. Charles de Bourbon himself was among them. In an act of bravura he had put a ladder up against the wall and started to climb, motioning for his troops to follow. He was struck down by a harquebus shell fired from above and died quickly. Benvenuto Cellini, the Florentine jeweler and sculptor, claims in his memoirs to have fired this shot. His veracity is questionable, but the account is lively and full of color, authentic at least for the general atmosphere of the morning's fighting:

"Bourbon's army had now arrived before the walls of Rome, and Alessandro begged me to go with him to reconnoitre. So we went with one of the stoutest fellows in our company; and on the way a youth called Cecchino della Casa joined himself to us. On reaching the walls by the Campo Santo, we could see that famous army, which was making every effort to enter the town. Upon the ramparts where we took our station, several young men were lying killed by the besiegers; the battle raged there desperately, and there was the densest fog imaginable. I turned to Alessandro and said: 'Let us go home as soon as we can, for there is nothing to be done here; you see the enemies are mounting, and our men are in flight.' Alessandro, in a panic, cried: 'Would God that we had never come here!' and turned in maddest haste to fly. I took him up somewhat sharply with these words: 'Since you have brought me here, I must perform some action worthy of a man'; and directing my arquebuse where I saw the thickest and most serried troop of fighting men, I aimed exactly at one whom I remarked to be higher than the rest: the fog prevented me from being certain whether he was on horseback or on foot. Then I turned to Alessandro and Cecchino, and bade them discharge their arquebuses, showing them how to avoid being hit by the besiegers. When we had fired two rounds apiece, I crept cautiously up to the wall, and observing among the enemy a most extraordinary confusion, I discovered afterwards that one of our shots had killed the [duke] of Bourbon; and from what I subsequently learned, he was the man whom I had first noticed above the heads of the rest."

The news of Bourbon's death greatly cheered the Romans, but it was in fact unfortunate because he was not to be present to moderate his troops when they took the city. The first of the enemy apparently came in through houses built in the walls, and then the walls themselves were breached in several places. Once the enemy had penetrated in force, the defenders lost courage and discipline and began to flee. The battle was lost.

Pope Clement was praying in Saint Peter's when Spanish soldiers entered the basilica chasing Swiss guardsmen. With the young historian Paolo Giovio, he hurried once again through the overhead passage to Castel Sant' Angelo. From all over the city refugees headed for the ancient castle fortress. There were eventually several thousand people inside, including thirteen cardinals. The drawbridge was finally pulled up. A latecomer, Cardinal Armellini (known for his greed), had to be hoisted up in a basket. The castle was not attacked systematically, for everyone considered it to be impregnable, but the refugees on the terraces were horrified witnesses of the carnage in the city below. Cellini, who had run to Sant' Angelo and been admitted, after leaving the city walls, rushed up to the battlements to see how he might make himself useful: "I attached myself to certain pieces of artillery, which were under the command of a bombardier called Giuliano Fiorentino. Leaning there against the battlements, the unhappy man could see his poor house being sacked, and his wife and children outraged; fearing to strike his own folk, he dared not discharge the cannon, and flinging the burning fuse upon the ground, he wept as though his heart would break, and tore his cheeks with both his hands."

Cellini then took charge of the situation and makes some characteristically immodest claims about his own accomplishments: "I aimed some swivels and falconets at points where I saw it would be useful, and killed with them a good number of the enemy. Had it not been for this, the troops who poured into Rome that morning, and were marching straight upon the castle, might possibly have entered it with ease, because the artillery was doing them no damage. I went on firing under the eyes of several cardinals and lords, who kept blessing me and giving me the heartiest encouragement. In my enthusiasm I strove to achieve the impossible; let it suffice that it was I who saved the castle that morning, and brought the other bombardiers back to their duty."

By noon all of the right bank of the Tiber—Vatican, Borgo, Trastevere—was in the enemy's hands except the castle itself. Then Ponte Sisto was attacked and crossed. Defending soldiers broke their formations, thinking only to the safety of their own houses—but it was of course folly to think single houses could be defended when the city was lost. The victorious invaders were held in some check during the day, being ordered into formations by their officers, but during the night they dispersed to pillage.

One of the characters in Aretino's *Ragionamenti* evokes the horrors of this first night of the Sack: "But then came the night . . . with the army from Trastevere spreading out through Rome; already cries are heard, doors crash to the ground, everyone flees, everyone hides, everyone weeps. Meanwhile blood bathes the streets, people kill themselves, the tortured scream, the prisoners beg, the women tear their hair, the elderly tremble, and, the city turned upside down, blessed is he who has died quickly or, in his agony, finds someone to despatch him—but who could tell the horror of such a night? Friars, monks, chaplains . . . armed or disarmed, flattened out to hide in the sepulchres, more dead than alive, nor was there a cave or a hole or a well or a tower or a cellar or any kind of secret place that was not immediately full of all kinds of persons. Respectable and prominent men were beaten, stripped of their clothes, mocked and spat upon. Neither churches, nor hospitals, nor private houses nor anything else was respected. These men went even into places where men must not enter [that is, convents], and they scornfully chased women into places [brothels] where every woman is excommunicated for entering. But the most pitiful thing was to see the fire in the golden loggias and in the frescoed palaces; the most grievous was to hear the husbands, red from the blood of their wounds, calling their lost wives with a voice which would cause to weep that marble stone of the Colosseum which holds together without mortar."

The first horrors had begun. Many people were killed quickly in madness and anti-Roman fury. Countless women were violated in their homes and convents or taken away to be abused elsewhere. Houses were burned for spite. Lines of soldiers passed through the streets carrying loot. Wealthy people were seized for ransom, and the Spaniards hit on the efficacious device of torturing the rich or, better, their wives and children, in order to make them tell where valuables were hidden.

At least ten days of general terror followed before the soldiers were brought under even approximate control, and the occupation of Rome lasted nine months, with sporadic outrages during the whole time. To the horrors of physical violence were soon added those of famine and plague. The number of dead from all causes among residents of the city may have been ten thousand, and another ten thousand departed when it became possible. By the end of the occupation, the population had shrunk, then, by about twenty thousand, or by nearly forty per cent. The loss in money and property cannot of course be calculated accurately, but it certainly ran into millions of *ducati*. And one million *ducati* was at that time an almost unimaginable sum. Rome was indeed a wealthy city, and its wealth consisted largely of just the sort of things vandals could lay their hands on—money, gold and silver, and portable works of art.

Though the invaders' governing desire was for cash, losses in works of art and scholarship were incalculable.

Paintings were often destroyed, the soldiers seeing no way to draw money from them quickly. Books and manuscripts perished in thousands, usually destroyed rather than stolen, though precious bindings were ripped off and taken away. In the libraries of private houses and in bookstores, countless books were torn up and then strewn about the streets. It is probable that a percentage of Romans literary works of the period perished *in all copies*. Some works of antiquity, not yet edited, may even have been destroyed in their only extant versions. The priceless Vatican Library itself was entered and occupied, with an undetermined number of books in its collection being lost. Church and government records, both at the Vatican and at the Campidoglio, were burned, used for horse litter, or strewn about the streets, and portions of European history were lost forever.

No social condition or economic class or political faction was spared from the horrors of the Sack. A half-dozen cardinals who had not managed to get into Castel Sant' Angelo were the object of extortions and violence. Cardinal Pompeo Colonna was in league with the Imperials, but when he arrived in the city on May 9, he found that his own palace, the magnificent Cancelleria, had already been looted. He afterwards accepted many guests under his protection and made a show of being grieved over the sufferings of Rome. Marc Antonio Altieri, the aristocratic old-fashioned Roman and statesman of the Campidoglio, was also a member of the Colonna party and a Ghibelline of sorts. He opened his house to the invaders but was mistreated nevertheless and forced to pay protection money. The German and Spanish soldiers were scarcely interested in political distinctions.

Of the famous Roman writers and artists of the time, several had the good fortune to be away from the City. Michelangelo was working on the Medici tombs in Florence (and he remained there after the city revolted against the Medici at the time of the pope's defeat). Bembo had gone to live in Padua. Castiglione was in Spain as Clement's ambassador to the emperor. His grief on learning the fate of Rome was boundless. Aretino was in Venice; his grief was not excessive. At the end of May he wrote a letter to Clement advising him to trust in the emperor's generosity, asserting, "In His Majesty there is no arrogance." This hypocritical epistle made the pontiff hate Aretino all the more. Paolo Giovio and Francesco Berni were safe in the Castello. So also, as we have seen, was Benvenuto Cellini. His services there were not confined to artillerymanship. The pope had him melt down two hundred pounds of precious objects of gold so that new coins could be struck. Cellini, who always took "pleasure in extraordinary sights," seems to have enjoyed the whole experience. After peace was signed, he left for Florence, his pockets full of money paid for his services.

A number of intellectuals and artists had the misfortune to be in occupied parts of the town. Baldassare Peruzzi, the architect of Saint Peter's, lost his property but saved his life by painting a portrait of the dead duke of Bourbon, probably using a death mask as a model. The Florentine painter Rosso fell into the hands of the *lanzichenecchi*, was stripped, and was forced to carry burdens through the streets before finally escaping to Perugia. The architect and sculptor Jacopo Sansovino lost all his possessions. Giammaria Giudeo dei Medici, favorite musician of Leo X, fell into the hands of the Spaniards and killed himself to escape torture. Angelo Colocci, poet and host of one of the city's principal *orti letterari*, lost everything, including a precious library. He managed to leave the city, after having paid ransoms twice. Johann Goritz, the beloved host and Maecenas to whom the anthology *Coryciana* had been dedicated, gained no favor by his Germanic (Luxemburger) nationality. His house was seized and he had to pay a great sum. He left Rome to return to Luxemburg but died en route.

Italian historians have always emphasized the fact that many of the *lanzichenecchi* were admirers of Martin Luther and that they came to Italy with the idea that Rome was a new Babylon deserving destruction. The Germans were perhaps the authors of most of the sacrilegious acts. Tombs in Saint Peter's, including that of Julius II, were profaned. Soldiers got themselves up in the costumes of high churchmen and mocked religious ceremonies. A soldier dressed as the pope and others dressed as cardinals put on a masquerade in front of the Castel Sant' Angelo. The "pope" blessed some wine and gave it to the others to drink. Sermons were preached and hymns were sung. At the end of the ceremony Luther was proclaimed pope. But if the Germans deserve the principal shame for sacrilege, the Spaniards must have it for physical brutality, and the Italian contingent of the invaders, accounts indicate, were worthy companions of the foreigners. The peasants from Colonna lands around Rome were especially ruthless, having suffered lately at the hands of the pope's soldiers.

There was, in the legal sense, no "conquest" of Rome, that is, no transfer of sovereignty. The temporal states of the Church were defeated in war, but not abolished. Clement doubtless feared for his own life, but in the event no attempt was made to storm Castel Sant' Angelo. The pope and thirteen cardinals lived there in security, though uncomfortably and on relatively spartan rations. (A devout old lady who tried to deliver some fresh lettuce for the pontiff was hanged by the Imperials in front of the castle.) In their terrible misfortune the minds of the besieged churchmen turned to spiritual duties, and religious services went on almost constantly. Clement surrendered to the enemy on June 5, a month after the fall of the city, agreeing among other things to pay the sum of 400,000 *ducati*. He remained for a time in the castle, retaining control of the upper part while the lower stories were occupied by Imperial troops. Then, on December 7, the pope escaped from the castle disguised as a peasant. This escape was almost certainly winked at by occupying forces, but it was seen by some Romans and by devout Catholics in other countries as a sort of miraculous deliverance. Charles V was himself glad to have the pope free again; his Spanish clergy had been making strong intercessions on behalf of the Holy Father. (Near the end of his life Charles was to retire to a monastery, largely out of remorse for the outrages of Rome.) Clement stayed for several months at Orvieto, conducting business and receiving ambassadors in conditions almost of poverty. In June, 1528, he moved to Viterbo. On October 6 of that year he finally returned to Rome.

It has long been customary to take the year 1527 as the termination of the High Renaissance in Italy. The Sack of Rome does come as near as any single calamity can to marking the end of an age. There was, of course, no absolute break with the past, even in Rome itself. The pope regained his city and even most of his international prestige. In 1530 he crowned Charles V emperor at Bologna amid great pomp, and in 1533 he married his young cousin Catherine dei Medici to the son of Francis I at Marseille in equally grand circumstances. The Church also seemed to recover from the disaster, and Clement was followed in 1534 by a truly great pope, Paul III.

The *urbs* regained its population and prosperity, and there was much new building. Michelangelo, who returned to the city from Florence in the 1530's, became the architect of Saint Peter's and he designed the magnificent new Piazza of the Campidoglio. A new style of architecture, partly heralded by Michelangelo, later grew up in the city and spread through a large part of the Christian world as the Baroque. *Roma Triumphans* held its position as artistic leader of Europe well into the seventeenth century. Literary life took up again as well, and the passion for classical antiquity continued. The spirit of Roman life was, however, generally changed. Everyone knew that the freedom of Italy, such as it had been or had been dreamed of, was lost for an indefinite period. And a more thoughtful Church, in the Counter-Reformation, looked back with mixed feelings on the High Renaissance and the light-hearted frivolities of the Age of Leo X.

Before abandoning the age, and after seeing the misfortunes that ended it, we should recall for a moment the optimism and fervor that characterized it at its peak. The French Comte de Gobineau, usually remembered for his unfortunate racial theories, caught the spirit of the time extremely well in a dramatic sketch called *Léon X*. In one scene a minor artist says panegyrically to Michelangelo: "I consider you [Michelangelo] to be a demi-god, and others think as I do. Don't frown, and let me go on. Every day, almost, one sees entertainments such as one has never contemplated before. Here in Rome, as in Florence, as in Venice, in Milan, in Bologna, in Naples, the grandiose inventions of the ancients in this kind of magnificence are largely surpassed. As for scholars, poets, writers, there is no lack of them. New ones are being produced incessantly: Sannazaro, Sadoleto, Bembo, Navagero, the inimitable, the sublime Ariosto, Bibbiena with his *Calandria* and Master Nicolò Machiavelli with his *Mandragola*."

"What better or more shall I say? Pope Leo X and his cardinals appear to my delighted imagination as equals of the great Jupiter and the gods of the Pantheon, and they also live in an Olympus infinitely more beautiful than that of their fabulous precursors, since this former Olympus had been appointed by old Coelus, a poor god without taste and without sophistication. . . . today it is we artists who have created the firmament, who are embellishing it, illuminating it every hour with admirable nuances, making it shine with sparkling stars. And I tell you that wherever you put your hand, wherever Master Raphael, Andrea del Sarto, Sansovino, Titian, and so many others, work, the result is immortal."

Michelangelo, of course, makes a cynical reply: "You talk too much, Granacci, and are blind, incapable of understanding the meanness of what charms you, and the profound weakness of these people who delight you and who are worth so little." But then Michelangelo was well known as a pessimist and a spoilsport.

APPENDIX

SUGGESTIONS
FOR HIGH RENAISSANCE TOURISTS
IN ROME

In the vast artistic and architectural wealth of the Eternal City, deriving from well over two thousand years of history, the tourist interested in the heritage of the High Renaissance may easily become bewildered. He may, in particular, find himself spending all his time on ancient and baroque monuments, both more numerous than those from our period. The following are, in my opinion, the most important things from the High Renaissance to see while visiting the city.

1. *Architecture.*
    a. Bramante's *Tempietto* in the courtyard of the church of San Pietro in Montorio. The finest jewel of High Renaissance architecture.
    b. The Farnese Palace, built for Cardinal Alessandro Farnese, later Pope Paul III. Now the French Embassy, currently open to visitors on Sunday mornings.
    c. The Villa Farnesina, in the Via della Lungara, formerly the Villa Suburbana of the banker Agostino Chigi. Designed by Baldassare Peruzzi and decorated largely by Raphael.

2. *Sculpture.*
   Michelangelo's *Pietà*, in Saint Peter's, and his *Moses*, in
   the church of San Pietro in Vincoli. The latter was designed for the tomb of Julius II.

3. *Painting.*
   a. Michelangelo's frescoes depicting scenes from the
      Book of Genesis on the barrel-vaulted ceiling of the
      Sistine Chapel. (His *Last Judgment,* on the altar wall
      of the Chapel, was done in 1534–41, shortly after the
      close of our period.) Access to the chapel is through
      the Vatican Museum.
   b. The Stanze di Raffaello in the Vatican Palace, espe-
      cially the Sala della Segnatura, which contains the
      celebrated *School of Athens* and three other allegori-
      cal frescoes depicting famous poets, theologians, and
      jurists. In adjacent rooms Raphael has portrayed
      Popes Julius II and Leo X in the figures of several
      popes of more distant times. Access to the Stanze is
      through the Vatican Museum.

4. *Miscellaneous.*
   a. The mutilated ancient statue called "Pasquino," on
      which satirical verses were hung during the Renais-
      sance. In the tiny Piazza di Pasquino, just off the
      Piazza Navona.
   b. The Castel Sant' Angelo, not greatly altered in its
      general appearance since it served as a refuge for
      the Pope during the Sack of Rome. It has a number
      of rooms, such as the chapel of Leo X and the bath-
      room of Clement VII, that were decorated for the
      Medici popes.

c. The Trastevere quarter, whose surviving medieval streets afford an impression of what the plebeian quarters of Rome looked like in the Renaissance.

BIBLIOGRAPHICAL NOTES

The most important of all books about Pope Leo X and his time in Rome was written in English. William Roscoe, a British Italophile who had already done a fine biography of Lorenzo the Magnificent, published *The Life and Pontificate of Leo the Tenth* in 1805. It is a rich and discursive work of some one thousand pages, written without the benefit of travel in Italy but with the help of many documents brought to England by friends (among them the celebrated Lord Holland). The work has the charm of old-fashioned humanistic scholarship and is a masterpiece, despite an evident bias in favor of its subject. It had immediate success and was translated into Italian, French, and German. The Italian edition, by Count Bossi, includes many additional documents in the appendix. There were several new English editions in the nineteenth century, but the book has long been out of print. A three-volume reprint of the 1853 edition has, however, been announced by the APS Press in New York for 1973.

The most important study of Rome in the whole period was written in German, but soon translated. This is Volumes VI, VII, and VIII of Ludwig Pastor's monumental

History of the Popes from the Close of the Middle Ages (40 vols., London, Kegan Paul, 1899–1953). Pastor's is a much more modern and systematic sort of history, somewhat less entertaining but rich and solid.

A major study with a focus close to my own appeared in France in 1912. Emmanuel Pierre Rodocanachi's *La Première renaissance. Rome au temps de Jules II et de Léon X* (Paris, Hachette), despite its title, covers the city's life through the Sack of Rome in 1527. Rodocanachi, some of whose other works on Rome in the Renaissance are listed below, is perhaps most interesting for the number of poignant anecdotes and personal stories he gathered from many sources. His work was not translated into English and is now out of print in French.

In Rome itself, a great amount of pertinent research was done in the late nineteenth and early twentieth centuries by a brilliant local antiquarian, Domenico Gnoli. A number of his many articles deal with Rome in or near the time of Pope Leo X. Most of these were gathered after his death by his son Aldo and published in a volume called *La Roma di Leon X* (Milan, Hoepli, 1938). Gnoli's accounts have an immediacy and a down-to-earth quality that come from everyday knowledge of specific locales and native skepticism. For him the Romans of the early sixteenth century are fellow townsmen rather than figures in European history. His book was not translated and is out of print in Italy.

There have been several studies of the Medici family, some of them in English and some still in print. Colonel George F. Young's *The Medici*, first published in 1909, is now available in the Modern Library collection. Ferdinand Schevill's more professional but shorter study of the same name is issued as a Harper Torchback. Marcel Brion's much more recent book also called *The Medici* is issued in English translation by Crown Publishers. Herbert M. Vaughan's *The Medici Popes*, issued by Methuen of London in 1908 is out of print but available in many public and most university libraries. E. R. Chamberlin's *The Bad Popes* (New York, Dial Press, 1969) contains, despite its prejudicial title, some eighty very perceptive pages on Leo X and Clement VII. (Mr. Chamberlin is also the author of an informative *Everyday Life in the Renaissance* [New York, Capricorn, 1967].)

Two major nineteenth-century studies of the Italian Renaissance in general, leading to an enormous revival of interest, are now in print and enjoy a continuing popularity among students of the period. Jacob Burckhardt's *The Civilization of the Italian Renaissance*, probably one of the most influential works of scholarship ever written, is issued in two Harper Torchback volumes. It has numerous references to our popes and the Roman society of their time. John Addington Symonds' various volumes on the Italian Renaissance are reprinted by Capricorn Books, New York. The volume entitled *The Fine Arts* is the most interesting for students of High Renaissance Rome.

There are no well-known literary works of the actual time that deal in a major way with life in Rome. Castiglione's *The Courtier* (a Penguin Classic) is, however, extremely informative of the intellectual tenor of the time, though it is set in quiet little Urbino, safe from the bustle of Rome. And, finally, it would be hard to recommend too enthusiastically those of Giorgio Vasari's *Lives of the Painters, Sculptors, and Architects* that deal with artists who lived in Rome. The four-volume Everyman's Library edition (New York and London, Dent and Dutton) has an exhaustive index that permits one to find all the references to artists and patrons and important projects.

In the course of this book I have quoted long passages from the following sixteenth-century works, in the indicated editions:

Aretino, Pietro. *La Cortigiana,* in *Opere di Pietro Aretino.* Ed. Massimo Fabi. 2nd ed. Milan, Carlo Brigola, 1881.
———. *Sei giornate: Dialogo della Nanna e della Antonia* (1534) *e Dialogo nel quale la Nanna insegna alla Pippa* (1536). (This work is better known as *Ragionamenti.*) Ed. Giovanni Aquilecchia. *Scrittori d'Italia,* No. 245. Bari, Laterza, 1969.

Bembo, Pietro. *Prose della volgar lingua,* in *Opere in volgare.* Ed. Mario Marti. *I Classici Italiani.* Florence, Sansoni, 1961.

Cellini, Benvenuto. *The Life of Benvenuto Cellini Written by Himself.* Edited and translated by John Addington Symonds. 2 vols. New York, Brentano's, 1906.

Delicado, Francisco. *La Loçana andaluza.* Ed. Antonio Vilanova. Barcelona, Selecciones Bibliófilas, 1952.

Erasmus, Desiderius. *Ciceronianus.* Tr. by Izora Scott and included in her *Controversies over the Imitation of Cicero. Teachers College, Columbia University Contributions to Education,* 35. New York, Teachers College, Columbia University, 1910.

Grassi, Paride de'. *Il diario di Leone X di Paride Grassi.* Eds. Pio Delicati and Mariano Armellini. Rome, Tipografia della Pace, 1884.

Le Saige, Jacques. *Voyage de Jacques Le Saige de Douai à Rome, Notre-Dame-de-Lorette, Venise, Jérusalem et autres saints lieux.* Ed. H. R. Duthilloeul. Douai, Adam d'Aubers, 1851.

Sanuto, Marino. *I Diarii di Marino Sanuto (MCCCCXLVI-MDXXXIII)* . . . *pubblicati per cura di Renaldo Fulin, Federico Stefani, Nicolo Barozzi, Guglielmo Berchet, Marco Allegri, auspice la R. Deputazione Veneta di Storia Patria.* 58 vols. Venice, F. Visentini, 1879–1903.

Valeriano, Piero. *La Infelicità dei letterati . . . aggiuntovi dialogo del Valeriano sulle lingue volgari.* Milan, Tipografia Malatesta, 1829.

Quotations of Martin Luther have been taken from Roscoe's *Life of Leo X*, above. All translations in the text, except those from Cellini, Luther, and Erasmus, are my own.

Following is a list of the most important other works consulted for this book:

Altieri, Marc Antonio. *Giuliano de' Medici eletto cittadino romano, ovvero il Natale di Roma nel 1513.* Ed. Loreto Pasqualucci. Rome, 1884.

Anon. *Feste in Campidoglio nel settembre 1513 per l'esaltazione di Giuliano e Lorenzo dei Medici a patrizi romani.* Ed. F. Cerasoli. Offprint from *Buonarroti*, 1891.

Aretino, Pietro. *Lettere: Il Primo e secondo libro.* Vol. I of *Tutte le Opere di Pietro Aretino.* Eds. Francesco Flora and Alessandro del Vita. Milan, Mondadori, 1960.

Bembo, Pietro. *Epistolarum Petri Bembi cardinalis et patricii veneti nomine Leonis X Pont. Max. scriptarum libri XVI.* Venice, 1611.

Boncompagni-Ludovisi, Ugo. *Roma nel Rinascimento.* 4 vols. Albano Laziale, Fratelli Strini, 1928–29.

Charles V. *Correspondenz des Kaisers Karl V*. Vol. I (1513–32). Ed. Karl Lanz. 1844; reprinted, Frankfurt, Minerva, 1966.

Cian, Vittorio. *Pasquino e pasquinate nella Roma di Leone X. Miscellanea della R. Deputazione romana di storia patria*. Rome, Nella sede della Deputazione alla Biblioteca Vallicelliana, 1938.

Cleugh, James. *The Divine Aretino*. New York: Stein and Day, 1966.

Coryciana, Blossius Palladius roiano Corycio lucumbergen. a libellis Iust. V.C.S.P.D. Impressum Romae Ludovicum Vicentinum et Lautitium Perusinum. Mense iulio MDXXXIII. In same volume: *Francisci Arsilli senogallicen. De poetis urbanis, ad Paulum Iovium libellus.*

De'Blasi, Giorgio. "Problemi critici del Rinascimento," in *Orientamenti culturali; Le Correnti*, I, 243–416. Milan, Carlo Marzorati, 1956.

Delumeau, Jean. *La Vie économique et sociale à Rome dans la seconde moitié du XVIe siècle*. 2 vols. Paris, E. de Boccard, 1957–58.

Devoto, Giacomo. *Storia della lingua di Roma*. Volume XXIII of *Storia di Roma*. Istituto di Studi Romani. Bologna, Licinio Cappelli, 1940.

Fabroni, Angelo. *Leonis X Pontificis maximi vita*. Pisa, Landi, 1797.

Fanelli. "Il Ginnasio greco di Leone X a Roma," *Studi romani*, Vol. IX (1961), 379–93.

Ferrajoli, Alessandro. *Il Ruolo della corte di Leone X (Rotulus familiae Leonis X)*. Rome, R. Società Romana di Storia Patria, 1911.

Giovio, Paolo (Paulus Jovius). Biography of Leo X in *Illustrium virorum vitae*. Florence, Torrentini, 1549.

Gnoli, Domenico. "Raffaello alla corte di Leone X," *Nuova antologia*, Vol. XIV (April 16, 1888), 577–97.

———. *Un giudizio di lesa-romanità sotto Leone X, aggiuntevi le orazioni di Celso Mellini e di Cristoforo Longolio.* Rome, Tipografia della Camera dei Deputati, 1891.

Gobineau, Comte Joseph Arthur de. *"Léon X,"* one of five *Scènes historiques* collectively called *La Renaissance.* Paris, Plon-Nourrit, 1908.

Gregorovius, Ferdinand. "Alcuni cenni storici sulla cittadinanza romana," *Atti della Reale Accademia dei Lincei, Anno CCLXXIV (1876–77)*; third series, *Memorie della Classe di Scienze morali, storiche e filologiche*, Vol. I, 314–46. Rome, Salviucci, 1877.

In Celsi Archelai Melini funere amicorum. Anthology of poems on the death of Celsi Mellini. No date or place of publication is given, but the volume was almost certainly printed in Rome in 1520.

Landucci, Luca. *Diario fiorentino al 1450 al 1516, continuato da una anonimo fino al 1542.* Ed. Iodoco del Badia. Florence, Sansoni, 1883.

Lauts, Jan. *Isabelle d'Este, 1474–1539.* Tr. from German by Germaine Welsch. Paris, Plon, 1956.

Madelin, Louis. "Le journal d'un habitant français de Rome au seizième siècle (1509–40)," in *France et Rome* (Paris, Plon, 1913), 197–262.

Meneghetti, Gildo. *La Vita avventurosa di Pietro Bembo, umanista-poeta-cortigiano.* Venice, Tipografia commerciale, 1961.

Navenne, Ferdinand de. *Rome, le Palais Farnèse et les Farnèse.* Paris, Albin Michel, n.d.

Palliolo, Paolo. *Le feste pel conferimento del patriziato romano a Giuliano e Lorenzo de' Medici, narrate da*

Paolo Palliolo fanese. Ed. O. Guerrini. Bologna, Romagnoli, 1885.

Paschini, Pio. *Roma nel Rinascimento.* Vol. XII of *Storia di Roma,* Istituto di Studi Romani. Bologna, Licinio Cappelli, 1940.

Pasquino. *Consigli utilissimi dello eccellente dottore nostro Pasquino a tutti li gentiluomini, officiali, procuratori, notari, artisti, bravazzi et altri che vengono di novo a Roma. Tradutti da greco in latino et de latino in vulgar. Novamente stampati.* Rome, Per Valerio Dorico, n.d. Probably published between the pontificate of Leo X and the mid-sixteenth century.

Pecchiai, Pio. *Roma nel Cinquecento.* Vol. XIII of *Storia di Roma,* Istituto di Studi Romani. Bologna, Licinio Cappelli, 1948.

Pirro, A. "Léon X et la musique," in *Mélanges de philologie, d'histoire et de littérature offerts à Henri Hauvette,* 221–34. Paris, Presses françaises, 1934.

Rodocanachi, Emmanuel Pierre. *Le Capitole romain antique et moderne.* Paris, Hachette, 1904.

———. Les *Institutions communales de Rome sous la Papauté.* Paris, Alphonse Picard, 1901.

———. *Le Saint-Siège et les Juifs; le Ghetto à Rome.* Paris, Firmin-Didot, 1891.

Sabbadini, Remigio. *Storia del Ciceronianismo e di altre questioni letterarie nell'età della rinascenza.* Turin, Ermanno Loescher, 1855.

Sadoleto, Jacopo. *Jacopi Sadoleti S.R.E. Cardinalis epistolae Leonis X Clementis VII Pauli III nomine scriptae.* Rome, Antonio Florevelli, 1759.

Sannazaro, Jacopo. *Actii Synceri Sannazaris neapolitani viri patricii De Partu Virginis etrusco carmine redditi a comite Bartolomaeo Casaregio.* Florence, Ex Tipographia Caietani Albizinii, 1740.

Sanzio, Raffaello. *Lettera di Raffaello d'Urbino a Papa Leone X, di nuovo posta in luce dal Cavaliere Pietro Ercole Visconti.* Rome, Tipografia delle Scienze, 1840.

Scott, Izora. *Controversies over the Imitation of Cicero as a Model for Style and Some Phases of their Influence on the Schools of the Renaissance. Teachers College, Columbia University Contributions to Education,* 35. New York, Teachers College, Columbia University, 1910.

Toffanin, Giuseppe. *Il Cinquecento. Storia letteraria d' Italia.* 6th ed. Milan, Vallardi, 1960.

Winspeare, Fabrizio. *La Congiura dei cardinali contro Leone X.* Florence, Olschki, 1957.

INDEX

Accolti, Cardinal Bernardo: 102, 112
Accursio (chamberlain of Julius II): 100–101
Acrone (Latin king): 64
Acropolis (Athens): 63
Acqueducts: 51
Adrian VI (pope): 122, 126–28; character of, 18–19
Aeneas: 64
Aeneid: 92
Africa (epic poem of Petrarch): 92
Agone (present Piazza Navona): 32, 75, 99
Agriculture: 53
Alexander VI (pope): 8–9, 16, 43, 61
Alexander the Great: 7
Alexandria, Egypt: 38
Altieri, Marc' Antonio: 40–41, 122–23, 138
Anne, Saint: 98
Anthony, Mark: 65
Apelles: 65
Apollo: 72, 99, 122
Aracoeli, church of: 36, 63
Aretino, Pietro: 47, 54–55, 86,
101–103, 119–22, 129, 136, 139
Ariosto, Ludovico: 74, 79, 102, 119, 143
Armellini, Cardinal: 135
Arsilli, Francesco: 98
Asolani (work of Pietro Bembo): 83
Athens: 16, 34, 63
Augustinians: 32
Augustus, Age of: 34
Avignon, France: seat of papacy in fourteenth century, 5

Banchi, Via dei: 42
Baraballo (archpoet): 90–91, 102
Baroque: 142, 145
Basel, Switzerland: 97
Beggars: 53
Bembo, Pietro (later cardinal): 81–83, 86–87, 91–92, 94, 102–104, 112, 122, 129, 139, 143
Berni, Francesco: 129, 139
Bernini, Gian Lorenzo: 23
Bibbiena: *see* Bernardo Dovizi
Boccaccio, Giovanni: 83

159

The Centers of Civilization Series, of which *Rome in the High Renaissance* is the thirty-third volume, is intended to include accounts of the great cities of the world during particular periods of their flowering, from ancient times to the present. The following list is complete as of the date of publication of this volume:

1. Charles Alexander Robinson, Jr. *Athens in the Age of Pericles.* (Also available in paper)
2. Arthur J. Arberry. *Shiraz: Persian City of Saints and Poets.*
3. Glanville Downey. *Constantinople in the Age of Justinian.*
4. Roger Le Tourneau. *Fez in the Age of the Marinides.* Translated from the French by Besse Alberta Clement.
5. Henry Thompson Rowell. *Rome in the Augustan Age.* (Also available in paper)
6. Glanville Downey. *Antioch in the Age of Theodosius the Great.*
7. Richard M. Kain. *Dublin in the Age of William Butler Yeats and James Joyce.*
8. Glanville Downey. *Gaza in the Early Sixth Century.*
9. Bernard Lewis. *Istanbul and the Civilization of the Ottoman Empire.*
10. Richard E. Sullivan. *Aix-la-Chapelle in the Age of Charlemagne.*
11. Elizabeth Riefstahl. *Thebes in the Time of Amunhotep III.* (Available in paper only)
12. Nicola A. Ziadeh. *Damascus Under the Mamlūks.*

13. Edward Wagenknecht. *Chicago.*
14. Arthur Voyce. *Moscow and the Roots of Russian Culture.*
15. Paul Ruggiers. *Florence in the Age of Dante.*
16. Gaston Wiet. *Cairo: City of Art and Commerce.* Translated by Seymour Feiler.
17. Douglas Young. *Edinburgh in the Age of Sir Walter Scott.*
18. Richard Nelson Frye. *Bukhara: The Medieval Achievement.*
19. Walter Muir Whitehill. *Boston in the Age of John Fitzgerald Kennedy.*
20. Arthur J. May. *Vienna in the Age of Franz Josef.*
21. John J. Murray. *Amsterdam in the Age of Rembrandt.*
22. Wendell Cole. *Kyoto in the Momoyama Period.*
23. Aldon D. Bell. *London in the Age of Charles Dickens.*
24. John Griffiths Pedley. *Sardis in the Age of Croesus.*
25. W. W. Robinson. *Los Angeles: A Profile.*
26. George C. Rogers, Jr. *Charleston in the Age of the Pinckneys.*
27. John J. Murray. *Antwerp in the Age of Plantin and Breughel.*
28. Gaston Wiet. *Baghdad: Metropolis of the Abbasid Caliphate.* Translated by Seymour Feiler.
29. William R. Tyler. *Dijon and the Valois Dukes of Burgundy.*
30. Barisa Krekic. *Dubrovnik in the Fourteenth and Fifteenth Centuries: A City Between East and West.*

31. Alec R. Myers. *London in the Age of Chaucer.*
32. W. N. Hargraves-Mawdsley. *Oxford in the Age of John Locke.*
33. Bonner Mitchell. *Rome in the High Renaissance.*

The paper on which this book is printed bears the watermark of the University of Oklahoma Press and has an effective life of at least three hundred years.